DECLARING
THE END FROM THE
BEGINNING

Revealing hidden patterns and meanings in Hebrew Scripture

Rose Peak & Mervyn Farrell

PUBLISHING
MASTERDESIGN
MAKING A DIFFERENCE ONE BOOK AT A TIME
SHERIDAN, WY

Master Design Publishing, an imprint of Master Design Marketing, LLC
30 N Gould St, Ste R
Sheridan, WY 82801
MasterDesign.org

ISBN Paperback: 978-1-941512-60-9
ISBN Ebook: 978-1-941512-61-6

10 9 8 7 6 5 4 3 2 1

Contents

Introduction vii

PART 1: PATTERNS OF NUMBERS AND HIDDEN CODING
    IN THE TANAKH
Chapter 1: Numerical Patterns in the Tanakh..............................3
Chapter 2: Hidden Meanings in the Tanakh 9

PART 2: PROPHECIES OF THE MESSIAH IN THE TANAKH
Chapter 3: TORAH The Law of Moses.................................17
Chapter 4: NEVIM The Prophets 25
Chapter 5: KETUVIM The Writings.....................................39

PART 3: LETTER TO THE SHOAH SURVIVORS
Chapter 6: God Is Old and Deaf and Goes on Holidays.................47

PART 4: MESSIANIC PROPHECIES IN SCRIPTURE
Chapter 7: The Book of Matthew 61
Chapter 8: The Book of Mark 77
Chapter 9: The Book of Luke 79
Chapter 10: The Book of John...85

PART 5: HIDDEN CODES AND NUMERICAL PATTERNS
    IN SCRIPTURE
Chapter 12: Yeshua Is Encoded in the Tanakh.....................95
Chapter 13: Numerical Patterns in New Covenant Scripture........99

PART 6: CONCLUSION
Chapter 14: In Summary...105
Chapter 15: How Do the Newly Discovered Facts Affect Us? 111
Chapter 16: Complete Salvation: Yshuwah or Sozo 131

Bibliography 135
Acknowledgments.. 137

Introduction

*T*HE HEBREW LANGUAGE AND the DNA of humans were planned to link up by our Creator God before He created anything. A link has been hidden in human DNA to reveal who the Creator was. Knowledge of this mystery was especially chosen for the times we live in, times of discovery of many hidden things made possible by the invention of, for instance, computers, microscopes, and the electron microscope, which enabled the discovery of DNA.

Scientists have found that there are four nucleic acids that form the basis of the DNA strand—adenine, guanine, cytosine, and thymine. The DNA chain of these four acids is attached by a sulfuric bridge. These bridges hold the DNA strand together and appear after ten acids, then after another five acids, another six acids, and then again after five acids, forming a repeating pattern of 10-5-6-5 within our DNA strand. Every letter in the Hebrew language is also a number; for instance, the first letter in Hebrew is aleph, which is also the number one, bet is the second letter, which is also the number two, and so on. Thus, this pattern within our DNA can be seen to spell a word. The number ten is the letter yod, five is heh, six is vav, and five is heh, which spells the Hebrew name for God given to Moses, YHWH, which means, "I am who I am" (see Heflin 2021). From this revelation comes the undeniable proof that there is only one true God, and that one is the Creator, and He has chosen to reveal Himself to us through the Hebrew language.

He is the God of the DNA, and He has signed His name in the Hebrew language into every cell of our bodies. His name is YHWH. He is the God of Abraham, Isaac, and Jacov. His name is embedded in our DNA. Now, just as every human has a fingerprint that is unique, never to be duplicated, so every human's DNA is unique, never to be duplicated. Therefore, our Creator is present at every human conception, giving unique DNA and fingerprints to that baby. Isn't this marvellous!

In this book we are trying to reveal to you miraculous proofs that the Tanakh (the Old Testament) is spoken by God, and men wrote down exactly what He said. There are three such proofs. The first proof involves straightforward mathematics, simply adding and multiplying to reveal the patterns of numbers hidden in the text. The second proof involves equal letter spacing, or ELS, in the Tanakh, which God allowed to be fully discovered with the invention of the computer. So, obviously, He saved the discovery of ELS for such a time as this. The third proof will be revealed to you later. But we will start with the first two.

Part 1

Patterns of Numbers and Hidden Coding in the Tanakh

Chapter 1

Numerical Patterns in the Tanakh

*P*ATTERNS OF NUMBERS AND hidden meanings that no human could duplicate have been discovered beneath the surface of the Tanakh. The Tanakh is like a large complex tapestry. If you look at the back of the tapestry, you see a lot of rough threads going in and out, but when you turn it over, you see the actual picture. We have been looking at the back of the Tanakh. We have not been looking at the right side and therefore have not discerned its hidden meanings and patterns. These hidden codes and patterns woven into the Tanakh have been identified in the last hundred years both with and without the aid of computers.

Running through the Tanakh are patterns of numbers that could not have been made by people. For instance, the number seven occurs in the Tanakh as it is in nature. It is well known that everything in nature runs according to mathematical laws. Nature is particularly marked by the number seven. Light from the sun consists of seven distinct colours—red, orange, yellow, green, blue, indigo, and violet. The earth is 49 times larger than the moon and 49 is 7 times 7, and the moon goes around the earth in 28 days or seven times four days. When looking at the gestation periods of animals, the number seven is again very prominent. The gestation period of the mouse is 21 (7 × 3) days; the rat's is 28 (7 × 4) days; the cat's is 56 (7 × 8) days; the dog's is 63 (7 × 9) days; the lion's is 98 (7 × 14) days; the sheep's is 147 (7 × 21) days; the chicken's is 21 (7 × 3) days; the common duck's is 28 (7 × 4) days; the golden eagle's is 35 (7 × 5) days; the emu's is 56 (7 × 8) days; the cassowary's and the kiwi's are both 42 (7 × 6) days. These are just to mention a few. Similarly, the gestation period for humans is 280 (7 × 40) days and the human body consists of 14 (7 × 2) elements. Our bodies are renewed in every cell every seven years.

Just as it occurs frequently in nature, the number seven runs through the Tanakh. The Sabbath is the seventh day of the week. The Hebrew people walked around Jericho seven times and the walls fell down and they captured the city. The seventh year in Hebrew law is a *Shemitah*, when the Jewish people were required to leave their fields fallow. It took seven years for the Jewish people to build the Temple in Jerusalem.

The number seven also occurs underneath the surface of the Tanakh, as discovered by Ivan Panin, a Russian scientist born in 1855. Take the first book of the Torah, Genesis, and look at Genesis 1:1. It reads, "In the beginning God created the heavens and the earth." It contains seven Hebrew words, and the number of Hebrew letters in the seven words is 28 (7 × 4). "In the beginning God created" has 14 letters (7 × 2). "And the heavens and the earth" also contains 14 letters (7 × 2). "God" is a subject of this verse and "heavens" and "earth" are its objects. The number of letters in the three Hebrew words is 14 (7 × 2). These are just a few of the patterns of sevens in Genesis 1:1. Panin (1934) lists fourteen instances of sevens in this first passage of the Tanakh and estimates that the probability of these occurring by chance is one in seven billion. Similarly, he found that all of the first five verses of Genesis 1 had many instances of sevens.

The number seven is also coded in the gematria of the words in Genesis 1. The "gematria" is the numerical equivalent of a letter, word, sentence, or passage. For instance, the first letter of the Hebrew alphabet is aleph, which is also the number one. The gematria of a word, sentence, or passage is the numerical value of the letters making up the text. In Genesis1:1, "God," "heaven," and "earth" are the significant nouns. "God" has a gematria of 86; "heaven" has a gematria of 395, and "earth" has a gematria of 296. If you add the gematria of these three words it comes to 777. The gematria of the word "created" in this verse is also a multiple of seven, being 203 (29 × 7). The value of the first, middle, and last words is 133 (19 × 7). If you take the first word in the verse and the last word and add the numeric value of their last letters, it comes to 490 (70 × 7) (Panin 1934).

The number seven also occurs in patterns of association, or chains, throughout the Tanakh. For instance, the number of writers of the Tanakh is 21 (3 × 7). If you add the gematria of these 21 names it totals 3,808 (544 × 7). The name David occurs in the Tanakh 1,134 (162 × 7) times (Sabiers 1941). Jeremiah's name occurs in seven books of the Tanakh, and the number of times it occurs is 147 (21 × 7). In Hebrew, Jeremiah's name occurs in seven different forms, the sum of the gematria of these forms being 1953, or 279 sevens. The first form of the name used has 273, or 39 sevens, and the last form of the name has 301, or 43 sevens. Of the 147 times that Jeremiah's name occurs, 14 (2 × 7) belong to its shortest form, and 126 (18 × 7) is the number of times the other six forms appear (Panin 1934).

An analysis of the numeric features of Genesis 5, the chapter of genealogies of the ten patriarchs before the flood, also gives evidence of patterns of sevens. Each patriarch is given three numbers: how old he was at the birth of his son, how long he lived after the birth of his son, and total years lived. The only number given for Noah is his age at his son's birth, so the genealogy includes just 28 (7 × 4) age numbers. The 28 numbers multiply to 15,750 (7 x 2 x 3 x 3 x 5 x 5 x 5), which is a multiple of seven with seven factors. Of the 28 numbers, seven are multiples of seven, and the sum of the seven numbers is also a multiple of seven. Panin (1934) identifies nineteen instances of sevens in the genealogy with impossible odds of this occurring by chance.

Panin found that many passages in the Tanakh had inexplicable numeric features often occurring on more than ten occasions. According to the law of probability, the possibility of the number seven being encoded in a passage on ten separate occasions is almost 1 in 3 million. Therefore, the possibility of humans writing these texts without supernatural inspiration is virtually nil. It seems reasonable that the numerical features of the Tanakh had been planned in advance. In the text of the Tanakh, it is many times written that God inspired the messages. For instance, ADONAI said to Jeremiah, "Behold, I have put My words in your mouth" (Jeremiah 1:9), and Adonai said to Ezekiel, "You will speak My words to them" (Ezekiel 2:7).

Chapter 2

Hidden Meanings
in the Tanakh

AN OBSERVATION WAS MADE by the scholar Michael Dov Weissmandl during the Second World War that there was mathematical coding or sequencing in the Torah (the first five books of the Tanakh). By selecting sequences of letters in the Torah, he found that a large number of meaningful words were hidden in the text. He found that the words occurred at equally spaced intervals, or *equidistant letter sequences* (ELS). There is evidence that prior to Rabbi Weissmandl, other rabbis from ancient times made reference to finding codes in Jewish Scripture. Researchers in Israel and the U.S. using high speed computers have tested the statistical probability of these codes and found that the probability of the Torah having these sequences is very, very small (see Witztum et al. 1994).

According to Professor Daniel Michelson (n.d.), by taking a letter in Scripture and skipping N − 1 Hebrew letters, and then identifying the Nth letter, then skipping N − 1 and identifying the next letter, and so on, many patterns have become evident in the Torah that are statistically improbable. For example, if you start with the first instance of the T in the book of Genesis, and skip 49 letters you come to the letter !. If you skip another 49 letters you come to R, and another 49 letters brings you to H. T!RH is TORAH. (It is interesting that the number 49 is a multiple of seven, being 7 × 7). Similarly, the word T!RH is spelled out by identifying every 50th letter from the first T in the book of Exodus. In the books of Numbers and Deuteronomy, T!RH is spelled backwards starting with H in the first verse of each respective book. So, in the first books of the Torah—Genesis and Exodus—TORAH is spelled out forwards, and in the last two books of the Torah—Numbers and Deuteronomy—it is spelled out backwards. The probability of TORAH being encoded in these books in such a way is approximately one in three million. TORAH is not spelled out in the central book, Leviticus, but the four-letter name of God, YHWH, is spelled out at equidistant spaces from the first letter in Leviticus.

One of the Israeli researchers, Professor Eliyahu Rips, found "Eden" encoded at equally spaced intervals sixteen times in Genesis 2:4–10, which describes the creation of the first man, Adam, and how God placed him in the garden called Eden (Jeffrey 1998). The ELS researchers found the names of the twenty-five trees referred to in the Tanakh encoded at equal intervals in Genesis 2, which describes the creation of man, woman, the plants, and the animals (Jeffrey 1998). Surprisingly, they also found the names of famous rabbis and their dates of birth and death encoded in the book of Genesis. The names and dates were encoded close to each other with minute probability of occurring by chance (Witztum et al. 1994). They also found that historic events concerning the Jewish people were encoded. For instance, in Deuteronomy 10:17–22, "Hitler," "Berlin," "Auschwitz," and "Belsen" are encoded. There is further encoding of the Holocaust identities, places, and events in Deuteronomy 31, 32, and 33 (Jeffrey 1998). Michelson (n.d.) reports that at the beginning of Leviticus, the book about the kohanim, the name of Aaron or AHRN, the kohen gadol, is coded 25 times with a probability of 1 in 400,000. These tiny probabilities of chance occurrence point to the divine inspiration of Hebrew Scripture.

Yacov Rambsel (2000) has done much research using ELS on Tanakh Scriptures (without the aid of computers) and made truly amazing discoveries. He looked at Genesis 1:22, "Then God blessed them by saying, 'Be fruitful and multiply.'" Counting from the third word and the first letter, 50 spaces forward spells the name of Avraham or Abraham. The name of Abraham's wife, Sarah, is also encoded here at 50 ELS. The probability of this encoding is about 1 in 10^8. Similarly, the names of Isaac and his wife, Rebekah, and Jacob and his wives, Leah and Rachel, are also encoded in Chapters 1 and 2 of Genesis.

> **Then God said, "Let lights in the expanse of the sky**
> **be for separating the day from the night. They will**
> **be for signs and for seasons and for days and years.**
> **They will be for lights in the expanse of the sky to**
> **shine upon the land." And it happened so. Then**
> **God made the two great lights—the greater light for**
> **dominion over the day, and the lesser light as well as**
> **the stars for dominion over the night. God set them**
> **in the expanse of the sky to shine on the land and to**
> **have dominion over the day and over the night and**

> **to separate the light from the darkness. And God saw**
> **that it was good. So there was evening and there was**
> **morning—a fourth day. — Genesis 1:14–19**

In these verses significant words are encoded at different ELS, some counting right to left and others left to right. Starting in Genesis 1:14, counting from right to left 19 letters from the first letter in the ninth word spells, "the South." In Genesis 1:14, counting from left to right from the fifth letter in the fifth word at 13 equal spaces reads, "the Bear." Adjacent letters to these read, "the Lion." Starting in Genesis 1:18, counting left to right from the first letter in the 11th word every 54 spaces reads, "Pleiades" (Rambsel 2000). Parallel to this, Job 9:9 reads, "He makes the Bear, Orion and Pleiades, and the constellations of the south," naming these constellations.

> **Then God said, "Let us make man in Our image, after**
> **Our likeness! Let them rule over the fish of the sea,**
> **over the flying creatures of the sky, over the livestock,**
> **over the whole earth, and over every crawling**
> **creature that crawls on the land." God created**
> **humankind in His image, in the image of God He**
> **created him, male and female He created them.**
> **— Genesis 1:26–27**

Looking at Genesis 1:26–27, the following words are identified at 17 letter intervals: "JHWH," "the Temple," "Man preserved," "in the light," and "created" (Rambsel 2000).

The text of Genesis 1:7 even has encoded the words for ELS: "So God made the expanse and it separated the water that was below the expanse from the water that was over the expanse. And it happened so." Counting left to right from the second letter in the 13th word every 14 letters spells "equally spaced intervals." Counting right to left starting with the fourth word and third letter at spaces of three letters spell, "codes of truth" (Rambsel 2000).

Rambsel (2000) noted that the name for ADONAI is spelled yod, heh, vav, and heh. The number for yod is 10, heh is 5, vav is 6, and heh is 5. The squares of these numbers are 100, 25, 36, and 25. When added together they equal 186. If you multiply 186 by 1000, it equals the speed of light! In Genesis 1:19, the words "heaven line of light" is spelled out at 5 letter spaces.

These facts below the surface of the Tanakh prove that it was divinely inspired and not merely the product of human thought and endeavour. In Rambsel's book, *The Genesis Factor*, he actually provides the probabilities of different words and phrases being encoded in the text of the Tanakh. In Isaiah 45:15, ADONAI says that He is God who hides Himself. In the ELS and patterns of numbers in the Tanakh, God has shown Himself to be a God of secrets, or hidden messages. Other hidden messages or mysteries of God are found in the prophecies of the Messiah in the Tanakh, which we now explore.

Part 2

Prophecies of the Messiah in the Tanakh

Chapter 3

TORAH
The Law of Moses

*I*N THE BOOKS OF the Tanakh, from Genesis to Deuter-onomy to Malachi, there is a clear message that the Messiah will come. In the following pages, we look at some of these prophecies of the Messiah, placing them in the context of authorship and historical period. We start with the Torah, or law of Moses, then look at the Nevim, or the prophets, and then look at the Ketavim, or writings.

THE BOOK OF GENESIS

The First Prophecy

I will put animosity between you and the woman—between your seed and her seed. He will crush your head, and you will crush his heel. — Genesis 3:15

The book of Genesis contains a prophecy of the Messiah that indicates that He would be the seed of a woman. The first man and woman whom ADONAI created were placed in a garden called

Eden to watch over it. ADONAI told them that they could eat from all the trees in the garden except the Tree of Knowledge of Good and Evil. However, the devil, God's enemy, also had access to the garden and his intentions were to destroy God's plan for the earth, especially His plan for the human race. The devil took the form of a serpent and deceived Eve, the woman, into eating of the forbidden fruit, and her husband followed her. Prior to this, the couple knew no sin. As a result, ADONAI increased the woman's pain in childbirth and cursed the ground so that the man's labour would be hard. ADONAI cursed the serpent so that it would crawl on its belly and eat dust. According to Genesis 3:15, in which God is talking to the devil, the Messiah would be the seed of a woman, rather than a man and a woman; the devil would injure the Messiah; and the Messiah would crush the devil's head.

Shem Is an Ancestor of the Messiah

Blessed be *ADONAI*, God of Shem, and let Canaan be his servant. May God enlarge Japheth, may he dwell in the tents of Shem, and may Canaan be his slave.
— Genesis 9:26–27

After the fall in the garden, sin and evil entered the human race. ADONAI saw that the intentions of people's hearts were bad and He regretted that He had made humankind. He decided to send a flood to destroy them. However, a man called Noah found favour with ADONAI because he was blameless. Thus, Noah and his family were spared. Noah fathered Shem, Ham, and Japheth. Ham had a son called Canaan. After the flood, Noah was in his vineyard and got drunk. Ham saw his father naked and told his two brothers, who covered their father without seeing their father's nakedness. Noah found out what had happened and declared that Shem was favoured by God and that Canaan, Ham's son, would be his slave.

The Messiah Descended from Abraham

Yes, I will establish My covenant between Me and you and your seed after you throughout their generations for an everlasting covenant, in order to be your God and your seed's God after you. — Genesis 17:7

One descendant of Shem's, Abram, originally came from Ur of the Chaldeans and was richly blessed by ADONAI. However, Abram had no descendants as his wife Sarai was barren. When Abram and Sarai were old, ADONAI promised them a son through whom would rise many nations. ADONAI, in a covenant act, changed Abram's name to Abraham, or father of many nations, and Sarai's to Sarah, or mother of many nations. Both Abraham and Sarah laughed at ADONAI, but He said, "Is anything too difficult for ADONAI?" (Genesis 18:13). He also said that His covenant was with Abraham and his descendants. Thus, the Messiah was to descend from Abraham.

The Messiah Descended from Isaac, Abraham and Sarah's Son

Whatever Sarah says to you, listen to her voice. For through Isaac shall your seed be called. — Genesis 21:12

Because Sarah was barren, she told Abraham to have relations with her maid servant, Hagar, who perhaps would bear him a son. Abraham took Hagar as his wife and she became pregnant and bore a son whom ADONAI instructed her to call Ishmael. However, true to ADONAI's promise, at an old age Sarah was given supernatural ability to conceive and give birth to the forerunner of the Messiah, who was Isaac, rather than Ishmael, Hagar's son. Hagar made fun of Sarah, so Sarah told Abraham to drive her away in order that Ishmael would not be an heir with Isaac. ADONAI said to Abraham not to be displeased about Ishmael and Hagar, as He would make the boy into a mighty nation. In Genesis 21:12, ADONAI, addressing Abraham, said to listen to Sarah, for God's covenant would be through Isaac.

The Messiah Would Be the Seed of Abraham

By myself I swear—it is a declaration of ADONAI—because you have done this thing, and you did not withhold your son, your only son, I will richly bless you and bountifully multiply your seed like the stars of heaven, and like the sand that is on the seashore, and your seed will possess the gate of his enemies. In your seed all the nations of the earth will be blessed—because you obeyed My voice.
— Genesis 22:16–18

But God tested Abraham and told him to sacrifice Isaac in Moriah on a mountain. Abraham took the knife to kill his son but ADONAI stopped him. ADONAI was pleased with Abraham's obedience. An angel of ADONAI declared the above message to

Abraham, that all nations of the earth would be blessed through a descendant of Abraham's.

The Messiah Would Be Descended from Jacob

Your seed will be as the dust of the land, and you will burst forth to the west and to the east and to the north and to the south. And in you all the families of the earth will be blessed—and in your seed.
— Genesis 28:14

Isaac married Rebekah. Rebekah bore twins, Esau and Jacob. Jacob deceived his father, Isaac, into getting the blessing due to Esau, his older brother. Thus, Jacob became heir of the promise. ADONAI appeared to Jacob in a dream. ADONAI was at the top of a stairway to heaven with angels going up and down the stairway. In the vision, ADONAI said to Jacob, as was said to Abraham before him, that all the families of the earth would be blessed through his seed.

The Messiah Would Descend from Judah

The scepter will not pass from Judah, nor the ruler's staff from between his feet, until he to whom it belongs will come. — Genesis 49:10

Jacob had twelve sons and just before he died in Egypt, he addressed each of his sons. When he addressed Judah, he indicated that the Messiah would be a descendant of his as expressed in this passage.

The Book of Exodus

Another Prophecy of the Messiah

You are not to carry the meat out of the house, nor are you to break any of its bones. — Exodus 12:46

Jacob's sons resided in Egypt where Joseph, a younger son, was a leader under Pharaoh. The Bnei-Yisrael multiplied greatly. However, a new king came to power in Egypt who was fearful that the Jewish people would war against the Egyptians, so he set slave masters over the Bnei-Yisrael and they were treated harshly. Pharaoh ordered that all the male Hebrew babies be killed by the midwives. Some of the babies, however, were spared by the midwives. One such baby was Moses, who was laid in a basket of reeds and put on the bank of the Nile. He was found by Pharaoh's daughter and she adopted him to be her son. He was brought up an Egyptian but was aware of his Hebrew ancestry. When Moses was older, he killed an Egyptian who tortured a Hebrew. In fear he fled to the land of Midian where he had an encounter with Adonai, who called Himself YHWH. Adonai sent Moses back to Egypt as His instrument to deliver His covenant people out of the cruel hand of the Egyptians. God sent many plagues against Egypt, but Pharaoh would not let the Hebrews go. So, Adonai instructed Moses to tell the Hebrews on a particular day to take a lamb, put its blood on the two doorposts and on the crossbeam of their houses, foretelling the Messiah. Adonai killed every firstborn male in Egypt, but the blood of the lamb was on the homes of the Hebrews and Adonai passed over them. Adonai said to Moses and his brother Aaron that at Passover the meat should be eaten but not be carried out of the house nor any of its bones be broken.

THE BOOK OF NUMBERS

Jacob Would Be the Messiah's Ancestor

For a star will come from Jacob, a scepter will arise from Israel. — Numbers 24:17

The Bnei-Yisrael passed through many nations to get to the land that God had promised them. One of these nations was Moab. The king of Moab, Balak, was terrified because Israel was so large in number and had conquered the Amorites. So, he sent men to summon Balaam, a prophet of ADONAI, to curse Israel. But God forbade Balaam to go with the Moabite men and an angel of ADONAI blocked the road. Balaam's donkey refused to move. Balaam repeatedly beat the donkey, but God enabled the donkey to speak and to ask Balaam why he beat her. Then Balaam saw the angel of God standing in the road and repented. Balaam did go to Balak, the king of Moab, but instead of cursing the Israelites, he blessed them and uttered an oracle. Part of this oracle was that a ruler would come from Jacob.

The Book of Deuteronomy

A Prophet Like Moses

Adonai your God will raise up for you a prophet like me from your midst—from your brothers. To him you must listen. — Deuteronomy 18:15

Before Adonai sent the children of Israel in to possess the Promised Land, He gave commandments to Moses, which Moses related to Israel. If the people kept the commandments, God would bless them, but if they disobeyed God, they would be cursed. As Moses was telling the people Adonai's plan and message, he declared that a prophet like himself would rise up from amongst them and they must listen to him.

Chapter 4

NEVIM
The Prophets

THE BOOK OF SAMUEL

The Messiah Would Descend from King David

When your days are done and you sleep with your fathers, I will raise up your seed, who will come forth from you after you, and I will establish his kingdom.
— 2 Samuel 7:12–13

The time came for the Bnei-Yisrael to enter the land that ADO-NAI promised to Abraham, Isaac, and Jacob, but Moses was not allowed to enter because he broke faith with God in the wilderness of Zin. Moses died in Moab aged 120 years and Joshua led the Israelites into the Promised Land. After Joshua's generation died, the Bnei-Yisrael started to worship non-gods or idols, so ADONAI let them be overtaken by their enemies. God raised up judges who saved them out of the hand of their many enemies. Living at the time of the judges was Hannah, a barren woman. ADONAI answered her prayer for a child and she conceived and bore a son, Samuel, whom she dedicated to the Lord. He became a prophet of ADONAI who led Israel against its enemies. His sons became judges over Israel. However, the people wanted a king to rule over them. They did not want God to rule directly over them. So, under ADONAI's direction, Samuel anointed Saul from the land of Benjamin as king over Israel. Saul reigned as king for forty-two years, but he feared the people and sought to please them instead of obeying ADONAI, so God gave the kingship to David, a young shepherd boy from Bethlehem. When David was king, ADONAI made a promise to him that He would raise up a great king from David's seed.

THE BOOK OF ISAIAH

After David, Israel had many kings, the first after David being his son, Solomon. After Solomon, his son Rehoboam reigned; however, the northern tribes rebelled against Rehoboam's rulership and declared independence, thus forming Israel. The southern state was Judah, which contained Jerusalem. Isaiah the prophet lived in Jerusalem during the reign of four kings of Judah around 3100 in the Jewish calendar, or 600 BC in the secular calendar. He had visions of and wrote frequently about the coming Messiah.

The Virgin Will Conceive

**Therefore, *ADONAI* Himself will give you a sign:
Behold, the virgin will conceive. When she is giving
birth to a son, she will call his name Immanuel.
— Isaiah 7:14**

One of the first of Isaiah's prophecies was that the Messiah would be conceived by a virgin, reminiscent of God's words to the serpent in Genesis 3:15 that the Messiah will be the seed of a woman.

The Messiah Will Be Both a Sanctuary and a Stumbling Block

He will be a Sanctuary, but a stone of stumbling and rock of offence to both the houses of Israel, a trap and a snare to the inhabitants of Jerusalem. — Isaiah 8:14

To many, the coming Messiah would be a sanctuary, a safe place, but to both houses of Israel, the Messiah would be a stumbling block to whom many would take offence. He would be a trap and a snare.

The Messiah Will Come from Galilee

But there is no gloom to her who was in anguish, as in time past. He treated lightly the land of Zebulun and the land of Naphtali, but in the future He will bring glory—by the way of the sea, beyond the Jordan— Galilee of the Gentiles. — Isaiah 8:23–24

Isaiah saw that the Messiah would come from Galilee beyond the Jordan in the region of the Tribe of Zebulun and the Tribe of Naphtali.

The Messiah Will Be a Light Shining in the Darkness

The people walking in darkness will see a great light. Upon those dwelling in the land of the shadow of death, light will shine. — Isaiah 9:1–2

Isaiah saw the Messiah as a great light that would appear to people walking in darkness and the shadow of death. This verse anticipates the hope for salvation and freedom that the Messiah will bring.

The Messiah Will Descend from David and Be an Everlasting Ruler

> For to us a child is born, a son will be given to us, and the government will be upon His shoulder. His Name will be called Wonderful Counselor, Mighty God, My Father of Eternity, Prince of Peace. Of the increase of His government and shalom there will be no end—on the throne of David and over His kingdom—to establish it and uphold it through justice and righteousness from now until forevermore.
> — Isaiah 9:6–7

Isaiah prophesied that a child would be given to Jewish people who at the same time would be ruler, counsellor, peace-bringer, and Almighty God. He would sit on the throne of David forever and be an everlasting ruler.

The Messiah Will Descend from Jesse

> Then a shoot will come forth out of the stem of Jesse, and a branch will bear fruit out of His roots. The *Ruach* of ADONAI will rest upon Him, the Spirit of wisdom and insight, the Spirit of counsel and might, the Spirit of knowledge and of the fear of ADONAI.
> — Isaiah 11:1–2

Isaiah prophesied that the Messiah would descend from Jesse, King David's father. The Messiah is a "branch" or *neh-tzer,* which can be interpreted "Nazarene." He will be mighty in the Holy Spirit, or the Ruach of ADONAI.

The Messiah Will Be a Cornerstone

Therefore, thus says ADONAI *Elohim*: Behold, I am laying in Zion a stone, a tested stone, a costly cornerstone, a firm foundation—whoever trusts will not flee in haste. — Isaiah 28:16

Isaiah refers to the coming Messiah as a cornerstone or a firm foundation, on the might of which the whole building of Zion will rest.

The Messiah Will Perform Miracles

They will see the glory of ADONAI, the splendor of our God. Strengthen the limp hands, make firm the wobbly knees. Say to those with anxious heart, "Be strong, have no fear!" Behold, your God! Vengeance is coming! God's recompense—it is coming! Then He will save you. Then the eyes of the blind will be opened and the ears of deaf unstopped. Then the lame will leap like a deer, and the tongue of the mute will sing. — Isaiah 35:2–6

Isaiah envisioned that in the time of the coming Messiah, the people would see the glory of ADONAI and that there would be great joy. God would save His people and this would be accompanied by mighty miracles.

The Messiah Will Be a Tender Shepherd

Look, *ADONAI ELOHIM* comes with might, with His arm ruling for Him. Behold, His reward is with Him, and His recompense before Him. Like a shepherd, He tends His flock. He gathers the lambs in His arms, carries them in his bosom, and gently guides nursing ewes. — Isaiah 40:10–11

Isaiah envisioned that the Messiah would be a tender, compassionate shepherd showing great love for His flock.

The Messiah Will Be Mighty in the Ruach

**Behold My servant, whom I uphold. My Chosen One, in whom My soul delights. I have put My Ruach on Him, He will bring justice to the nations. He will not cry out or raise His voice, or make His voice heard in the street. A bruised reed He will not break. A smoldering wick He will not snuff out.
— Isaiah 42:1–3**

In this passage, again Isaiah sees that the Ruach of God will be with the Messiah mightily and, again, that He will be tender and compassionate, especially to the weak and broken.

The Messiah Will Be a Light to the Nations

**So I will give you as a light to the nations, that You should be My salvation to the end of the earth.
— Isaiah 49:6**

In this passage, Isaiah declares that the Messiah will be a light to the nations and that salvation through Him will reach to the ends of the earth. Salvation will not be only for the Jewish race but available to all humanity.

The Messiah Will Be Tortured

I gave My back to those who strike, and My cheeks to those pulling out My beard; I did not hide My face from humiliation and spitting. — Isaiah 50:6

Although a light to the nations, Isaiah sees that the Messiah will be flogged, tortured, and humiliated.

People Will Not Acknowledge the Messiah

Who has believed our report? To whom is the arm of ADONAI revealed? — Isaiah 53:1

This passage speaks of the reluctance of the people to acknowledge the coming Messiah.

The Messiah Will Be a Sin-Bearer

Surely He has borne our griefs and carried our pains. Yet we esteemed Him stricken, struck by God, and afflicted. But He was pierced because of our transgressions, crushed because of our iniquities. The chastisement for our shalom was upon Him, and by His stripes we are healed. — Isaiah 53:4–5

This prophesy foretells that the Messiah will bear our griefs, pains, and sin. He will be pierced and scourged. Thus, the Messiah was pierced, suggesting that the form of execution was not stoning as was typically done in Israel. The word for "griefs" (derived from *chalah*) can variously mean anxiety, calamity, disease, or grief.

The Messiah Will Bear Our Iniquities

> We all like sheep have gone astray. Each of us turned
> to his own way. So ADONAI has laid on Him the
> iniquity of us all. . . . like a lamb led to the slaughter,
> like a sheep before its shearers is silent, so He did not
> open His mouth. — Isaiah 53:6

The Messiah will be killed like an animal but will not resist or try to defend Himself. He will bear our iniquity. The word for "iniquity" (*avon*) often refers to the consequences of idol worship. In Leviticus 16:21, the priest laid hands on the head of a live goat and confessed over it all the iniquities of the Israelites, all their transgressions and their sins. The goat was then sent away into the wilderness.

The Messiah Will Be Buried with the Rich

> His grave was given with the wicked, and by a rich
> man in His death. — Isaiah 53:9

Although the Messiah will be treated like an animal, He will be buried with the rich and affluent.

The Messiah Will Live

> Therefore I will give Him a portion with the great,
> and He will divide the spoil with the mighty—
> because He poured out His soul to death, and was
> counted with transgressors. — Isaiah 53:12

Isaiah sees that the Messiah will die, but He will live, as ADONAI will give Him a portion with the great as a reward for bearing our transgressions.

The Ruach Rests on the Messiah

> The Ruach of *ADONAI ELOHIM* is on me, because *ADONAI* has anointed me to proclaim Good News to the poor. He has sent me to bind up the broken-hearted, to proclaim liberty to the captives, and the opening of the prison to those who are bound, to proclaim the year of *ADONAI's* favour.
> — Isaiah 61:1–2

In this passage, Isaiah prophesies again that the Ruach of God is on the Chosen One. The anointing is especially for the poor, the broken, and the imprisoned.

THE BOOK OF JEREMIAH

Jeremiah was a prophet in Judah around 3300 of the Jewish calendar, or 450 BC, a very turbulent period of Jewish history when the tiny nation of Judah was threatened by Assyria, Babylon, and Egypt. However, Jeremiah saw hope in the coming Messiah.

The Messiah Will Be a Branch

> "Behold, days are coming" —it is a declaration of *ADONAI*—"when I will raise up for David a righteous Branch, and He will reign as king wisely, and execute justice and righteousness in the land. In His days Judah will be saved, and Israel will dwell in safety;

and this is His Name by which He will be called:
ADONAI our righteousness." — Jeremiah 23:5–6

In this passage by Jeremiah, as in the writings of Isaiah, the Messiah is referred to as a "branch."

There Will Be Mass Killing of Children

Thus says *ADONAI*: "A voice is heard in Ramah—
lamentation and bitter weeping—Rachel weeping
for her children, refusing to be comforted for her
children, because they are no more."
— Jeremiah 31:14

Jeremiah saw ahead a slaughter of innocent children.

There Will Be a New Covenant

"Behold, days are coming"—it is a declaration of
ADONAI—"when I will make a new covenant with the
house of Israel and with the house of Judah—not like
the covenant I made with their fathers in the day I
took them by the hand to bring them out of the land
of Egypt. For they broke My covenant, though I was
a husband to them." it is a declaration of *ADONAI*.
"But this is the covenant I will make with the house
of Israel after those days"—it is a declaration of
ADONAI—"I will put My Torah within them. Yes, I
will write it on their heart. I will be their God and
they will be My people. No longer will each teach
his neighbour or teach his brother, saying: 'Know
ADONAI,' for they will all know Me, from the least of
them to the greatest." It is a declaration of *ADONAI*.

"For I will forgive their iniquity, their sin I will remember no more." — Jeremiah 31:30–33

Jeremiah had hope for a new beginning. People seemed unable to keep the law of Moses. They continually turned to worshipping idols rather than placing their trust in God. Jeremiah saw ahead a new covenant that would not involve slavish observance of rules but would be written in people's hearts, which would be transformed by the power of God. The new covenant would involve the forgiveness of sin and iniquity. An inner holiness and strength would empower people to be faithful to God. God would be tangible and very close to even the least of them.

THE BOOK OF HOSEA

Hosea was a prophet in Israel, the northern kingdom, at the same time as Isaiah. In Hosea's time, Jewish people were increasingly turning to pagan gods.

The Messiah Will Be Called Out of Egypt

"When Israel was a youth I loved him, and out of Egypt I called My son." — Hosea 11:1

In this passage by Hosea, the Messiah is again called God's Son. He will dwell in Egypt from whence God calls Him.

THE BOOK OF MICAH

Micah was also a contemporary of Isaiah and lived in Judah. He denounced Samaria and Judah for their idolatry, but he saw redemption through the coming Messiah.

The Messiah Will Be Born in Bethlehem

But you Bethlehem Ephrathah—least among the
clans of Judah—from you will come out to Me One to
be ruler in Israel, One whose goings forth are from
of old, from days of eternity. Therefore He will give
them up until the time when she who is in labor has
given birth. Then the remnant of His brothers will
return to Bnei-Yisrael. So, He will arise and tend His
flock with the strength of *ADONAI*—in the majesty of
the Name of *ADONAI* His God. — Micah 5:1–3

Micah prophesied that the coming Messiah would be born in Bethelehem.

THE BOOK OF ZECHARIAH

Zechariah lived in the southern kingdom at the time of the construction of the second Temple, or in the 4th century BC. Zechariah was a visionary who prophesied repeatedly of the coming Messiah.

The Messiah Will Be a Branch

"Thus says *ADONAI-Tzva'ot*: Behold, a man whose
Name is the Branch will branch out from his place
and build the Temple of *ADONAI*. He will build the
Temple of *ADONAI*. He will bear splendor and sit and
rule on His throne." — Zechariah 6:12–13

As did Isaiah and Jeremiah, Zechariah named the Messiah "the Branch."

The Messiah Rides on a Donkey

Rejoice greatly, daughter of Zion! Shout, daughter
of Jerusalem! Behold, your king is coming to you, a
righteous one brings salvation. He is lowly, riding on
a donkey—on a colt, the foal of a donkey.
— Zechariah 9:9

In this passage, the prophet sees the Messiah entering Jerusalem
riding on a donkey's colt.

The Messiah Is Deemed Worthy of Thirty Pieces of Silver

Then I said to them, "If it seems good to you, pay me
my wages, but if not, don't bother!" So, they weighed
out my wages—30 pieces of silver. Then ADONAI said
to me, "Throw it to the potter—that exorbitant price
at which they valued Me!" So, I took the 30 pieces of
silver and threw them into the House of ADONAI, to
the potter. — Zechariah 11:12–13

Zechariah saw that the Messiah would be deemed to be worth
only thirty pieces of silver, which would be thrown to the potter.

The Messiah Will Be Pierced

"Then I will pour out on the house of David and
the inhabitants of Jerusalem a spirit of grace and
supplication, when they will look toward Me whom
they pierced. They will mourn for him as one mourns
for an only son and grieve bitterly for him, as one
grieves for a firstborn." — Zechariah 12:10

As Isaiah envisioned before him, Zechariah saw that the Messiah would be pierced and killed.

The Messiah's Followers Will Be Scattered

Strike the shepherd and the sheep will be scattered!
— Zechariah 13:7

In this passage, the prophet sees that the Shepherd will be attacked and that His followers will scatter.

THE BOOK OF MALACHI

Malachi lived at the time of the construction of the second Temple in Jerusalem. His name means "messenger," and he prophesied that a messenger would go before Messiah, who would come to His Temple.

The Messiah Will Come to His Temple

"Behold, I am sending My messenger and he will
clear the way before Me. Suddenly He will come to
His Temple—the Lord whom you seek—and the
Messenger of the covenant—the One whom you
desire—behold, He is coming," says *ADONAI-Tzva'ot*.
— Malachi 3:1

Chapter 5

KETUVIM
The Writings

THE BOOK OF PSALMS

The Messiah Will Be God's Son

**I will declare the decree of *ADONAI*. He said to me:
"You are My Son—today I have become Your Father."
— Psalm 2:7**

In this psalm, the Messiah is revealed as God's Son who will receive the nations of Earth as His inheritance.

Infants Praise ADONAI

**Out of the mouths of babes and toddlers You
established power. — Psalm 8:3**

In this psalm of praise, David foretells that the power of praise will be shown through infants.

The Messiah Will Live

**For You will not abandon my soul to Sheol nor let
Your faithful one see the Pit. — Psalm 16:10**

Many of the psalms were written by King David. Often, he seems to be writing prophetically—not about his own life but of someone else. In this psalm, it is predicted that the Messiah will not experience corruption either physically or spiritually.

The Messiah Experiences Abandonment by God

**My God, my God, why have You forsaken me?
— Psalm 22:2–3**

Psalm 22 is a psalm of David. It becomes obvious that David was not talking about a sickness he suffered but of a brutal execution echoing the 53rd chapter of Isaiah. Verses 2 to 3 speak of God's silence and abandonment during the depths of suffering at death.

The Messiah Will Be Taunted by Others

**"Rely on ADONAI! Let Him deliver him! Let Him
rescue him—since he delights in Him!"
— Psalm 22:9**

The person that David writes about is despised. He is taunted by others because he trusts God who has not saved him from a cruel death.

The Messiah's Executioners Divide His Clothes and Gamble for His Tunic

**My heart is like wax—melting within my innards. My
strength is dried up like a clay pot, my tongue cleaves**

**to my jaws. You lay me in the dust of death. For dogs
have surrounded me. A band of evildoers has closed
in on me. They pierced my hands and my feet. I can
count all my bones. They stare, they gape at me. They
divide my clothes among them, and cast lots for my
garment. — Psalm 22:15–19**

In this passage, David sees that the heart of the person being
killed is melted within him and his strength is gone. His hands
and his feet are pierced and he looks down at his body and counts
all his bones. His executioners divide his clothes and gamble for
his garment.

The Messiah's Bones Will Not Be Broken

**He keeps all his bones—not one of them is broken.
— Psalm 34:21**

This psalm, also by King David, echoes Passover. Not one of the
Messiah's bones will be broken.

Betrayal

**Even my own close friend, whom I trusted, who ate
my bread, has lifted up his heel against me.
— Psalm 41:10**

David, perhaps speaking prophetically, says that the Messiah is
betrayed by a close friend.

The Messiah Will Have Many Enemies

**Those who hate me without a cause outnumber the
hairs on my head. — Psalm 69:5**

In this psalm, David foretells that the Messiah will have innumerable enemies.

The Messiah Will Be Given Vinegar to Drink

Scorn has broken my heart, so I am sick. I looked for sympathy, but there was none, for comforters, but found none. They put gall in my food, and for my thirst they gave me vinegar to drink.
— Psalm 69:21–22

In these verses, David also envisions a broken heart. The suffering victim has no comforters and is given gall and vinegar to drink.

The Messiah Will Speak in Parables

I will open my mouth with a parable. — Psalm 78:2

This verse intimates that the Messiah will speak in parables.

The Messiah Will Descend from Judah

Then He detested Joseph's tent and chose not the tribe of Ephraim. Instead, He chose the tribe of Judah, Mount Zion, which He loved. — Psalm 78:67–68

In this psalm by Asaph, God chooses the tribe of Judah above the other tribes, echoing His message to Jacob in Genesis 49:10.

The Messiah Will Sit at God's Right Hand

ADONAI declares to my Lord: "Sit at My right hand until I make your enemies a footstool for Your feet."
— Psalm 110:1

According to Psalm 110, the Messiah will sit at God's right hand.

THE BOOK OF DANIEL

Daniel was in exile in Babylon from Judea, living after the destruction of the first Temple in the 5th and 4th century BC. Daniel sees history as fulfilling the purpose of God.

The Messiah Will Be Killed before the Temple Is Destroyed

> Then after the 62 weeks Mashiach will be cut off and have nothing. Then the people of a prince who is to come will destroy the city and the sanctuary.
> — Daniel 9:26

In Daniel's vision, he saw that the prince, the Messiah, would be killed before the destruction of Jerusalem and the Temple, which occurred in 70 AD.

THE BOOKS OF CHRONICLES

The books of Chronicles document Jewish history between the events recorded in the book of Judges and the exile in Babylon.

The Messiah Will Descend from King David

> It will be that when your days are fulfilled to go with your fathers, I will raise up your offspring after you, one of your own sons and I will establish his kingdom. He will build a house for Me and I will establish his throne forever. . . . I will appoint him over my House and My kingdom forever, and his throne will be established forever.
> — 1 Chronicles 17:11–14

In this passage from First Chronicles, ADONAI revealed to David that one of his descendants would be an everlasting ruler, making David an ancestor of the Messiah.

Thus, in Hebrew Scripture there are many references to the coming Messiah, some generally about His character and ministries and others more specific; for instance, details of His betrayal, death, and burial. References to His genealogy are also very detailed. Although God hides things, He also reveals things, although only in part.

Part 3

Letter to the Shoah Survivors

Chapter 6

God Is Old and Deaf and Goes on Holidays

*T*HE FOLLOWING IS A letter that I (Rose Peak) addressed to Shoah survivors. I worked with survivors for five years as an aged care worker and spent hundreds of hours talking to them about their lives during and since the war. There was a common thread in our conversations. The survivors couldn't understand why God had allowed the Holocaust to happen. Some said He was old. Some said He was deaf. Others said He went on holidays. For your loved ones and community to be persecuted and killed by an evil regime is one thing. But to feel abandoned by the One who made you would make life pointless and futile. For many of my clients who did have a strong faith, even their relationships with God were mixed with doubt, ambivalence, and sadness. Because of my position as a worker for a home care agency, I wasn't allowed to say much, but throughout those five years, I almost burst with a longing to respond and often went home in tears. The following section is dedicated to those survivors with whom I wasn't allowed to share my beliefs because of professional ethics and to all Shoah survivors who wonder why it happened.

THE DEVIL AND HIS FOLLOWERS

The Tanakh has a lot to say about evil: evil people, and the evil one himself, Satan or Lucifer. A psalm of Asaph reads:

> **They have none of humanity's trouble, nor are they plagued like others. Therefore, they put on pride as a necklace, and violence wraps around them like a garment. Their eyes bulge out from fatness. The imaginations of their hearts run wild. They scoff and wickedly plan evil. — Psalm 73:5–8**

An apt description of the Nazis. Evil people take on the nature of the evil one. The prophet Isaiah said of Satan,

> **How you have fallen from heaven, O brighstar, son of the dawn. How you are cut down to the earth, you who made the nations prostrate! You said in your heart: "I will ascend to heaven, I will exalt my throne above the stars of God. . . . I will make myself like Elyon." Yet you will be brought down to Sheol, to the lowest parts of the Pit. — Isaiah 14:12–15**

So, Satan was originally from heaven, but he was cast to Earth for wanting to make himself God. His destiny is the Pit. Ezekiel, the prophet, said of Satan that he was full of wisdom and perfect in beauty, perfect in his ways, and placed on the holy mountain of God until unrighteousness was found in him (see Ezekiel 28:12-15). Satan is very real and at large on planet Earth, and he hates all that God loves, especially you, God's chosen. But in Genesis God promised an answer. The first man and woman were given dominion over the earth as described in Genesis 1, verses 26 and 27. However, the devil beguiled them and so dominion over the earth went to the devil. When God was talking to the devil after the Fall in the Garden of Eden, He promised that He would put animosity between the devil and the woman—between its seed and the woman's seed.

"He will crush your head, and you will crush his heel."
— Genesis 3:15

God promised redemption. He said that a descendent of the woman would defeat the devil. ADONAI said to Moses, as recorded in Deuteronomy 18, that He

"will raise up a prophet like you for them from
among their brothers. I will put my words in his
mouth, and he will speak to them all that I command
him." — Deuteronomy 18:18

These Scriptures told of the coming Messiah. Isaiah also foretold of the coming Messiah. He said that He would not be beautiful but that

He was despised and rejected by men, a man of
sorrows, acquainted with grief, One from whom
people hide their faces. — Isaiah 53:3

He said that the Messiah would bear the people's griefs and carry their sorrows. And He would

be pierced because of our transgressions, crushed
because of our iniquities. — Isaiah 53:5

So, God would send the Messiah who would not only defeat the devil but also be a sin-bearer. There are many references by the Hebrew prophets to the Messiah, from Moses around 2440 in the Jewish calendar (1300 BC) to Malachi at the time of the second Temple. I have studied these prophecies in depth and would like to share some of them with you. Many of them were not general prophecies but specific details of the coming Messiah's conception, birth, ancestry, life, death, and resurrection. Many of these prophecies were through King David. David said that the Messiah would be betrayed—

> Even my own close friend, whom I trusted, who ate
> my bread, has lifted up his heel against me.
> — Psalm 41:10

The price for His betrayal was foretold by the prophet Zechariah, who said that the money would be cast to the potter.

> Then I said to them, "If it seems good to you, pay me
> my wages, but if not, don't bother." So, they weighed
> out my wages—30 pieces of silver. Then ADONAI said
> to me, "Throw it to the potter—that exorbitant price
> at which they valued me!" — Zechariah 11:12–13

Isaiah prophesied that the Messiah would be scourged:

> I gave My back to those who strike, and My cheeks to
> those pulling out My beard. — Isaiah 50:6

And King David writing 3000 years ago wrote graphically about the Messiah's death—

> For dogs have surrounded me. A band of evildoers
> has closed in on me. They pierced my hands and my
> feet. I can count all my bones. — Psalm 22:17–18

David also prophesied in Psalm 22 that the Messiah's clothes would be gambled for.

> **They divide my clothes among them and cast lots for**
> **my garment. — Psalm 22:19**

And in Psalm 69 David foretold—

> **For my thirst they gave me vinegar to drink.**
> **— Psalm 69:22**

JESHUA

Compare the writings of Zechariah with those of Matthew, the author of one of the gospels of Jeshua. He said that Jeshua was betrayed for 30 shekels of silver (Matthew 26:15) and that Judas, His betrayer, feeling remorse tossed the silver into the sanctuary and hung himself and that the ruling kohanim and elders bought the potter's field with the money (Matthew 27:1-4). Fulfilling Isaiah's prophecy, Jeshua was scourged, and fulfilling King David's Psalm 22, His hands and His feet were pierced during crucifixion. Because His body was naked and exposed during crucifixion, He could see all His bones. True to David's prophecy, Jeshua's clothes were gambled for. John the apostle wrote that the Roman soldiers who killed Jeshua said to one another about Jeshua's tunic:

> **Let's not tear it but cast lots for it to see whose it will**
> **be. — John 19:24**

True to David's prophecy in Psalm 69 that the Messiah would be given vinegar, John wrote of the time of Jeshua's death:

> **"I am thirsty." A jar full of sour wine was sitting there,**
> **so they put a sponge soaked with the sour wine on a**
> **hyssop branch and brought it to His mouth. When**

Jeshua tasted the sour wine, He said, "It is finished."
And He bowed His head and gave up His spirit.
— John 19:28–30

There are over 300 Hebrew prophecies fulfilled in the life of Jeshua. The genealogy of Jeshua in Matthew says that he was a descendent of Abraham, Isaac, Jacob, Judah, Jesse, David, and Solomon, all predicted in detail in Jewish Scripture. Micah prophesied that He would be born in Bethlehem Ephrathah. Hosea prophesied that He would be called out of Egypt when He was a child. And Isaiah said that there would come forth a rod out of the stem of Jesse and a branch would grow out of his roots. The word "branch" is regarded as a messianic title. In Hebrew, "branch" is *netser* from which Nazara or Nazareth is derived. Even this apparent contradiction is explained in Jeshua's life. Jeshua was born in Bethlehem, went to Egypt with His parents, and returned to Nazareth to live. As spoken of by Isaiah, Jeshua was a sin-bearer. His cousin, John the Baptist, said that He was the Lamb of God who takes away the sins of the world. Isaiah in chapter 53 also spoke that the Messiah would live after death.

> **Yet it pleased ADONAI to bruise Him. He caused Him**
> **to suffer. If He makes His soul a guilt offering, He**
> **will see His offspring, He will prolong His days.**
> — Isaiah 53:10

In Psalm 16, David said of the Messiah that God would not leave His soul in Sheol or suffer the Holy One to see corruption. All four of the gospel writers attest that Jeshua appeared to His disciples after death. The gospel writer Luke said that Jeshua said to His followers,

**"Look at My hands and My feet—It is I myself! Touch
Me and see! For a spirit doesn't have flesh and bones,
as you see I have." — Luke 24:19**

Isaiah (52:15) said that the Messiah would sprinkle many nations. True to this prophecy, the knowledge of Jeshua has gone
all around the world. He came first for the Jewish people but was
also a light to the Gentiles. Jeshua said that Satan was the ruler
of this world (John 14:30). The devil actually killed Jeshua but it
was through His death that He offered salvation not only to the
Jewish race from which He came, but to all humankind.

Protection Is through Jeshua

He took our sins on Himself. But more than that, He promises
protection from evil.

**For this reason was the Son of God manifested, that
He might destroy the works of the devil.
— 1 John 4:8**

**Having disarmed principalities and powers, He made
a public spectacle of them, triumphing over them in
the cross. — Colossians 2:15**

Yeshua said of Himself,

**"All authority has been given to Me in heaven and on
earth." — Matthew 28:18**

What I longed to tell my clients was that protection is through
Yeshua. He is the Protector and Redeemer of Israel. He loves
you. He didn't stand back and "allow" the Holocaust to happen. God has bound Himself to His original plan. Adam and

Eve originally had dominion over the earth (Genesis 1:26–28). However, they sinned by obeying Satan and consequently gave their authority over the earth to the evil one. Through Yeshua, our authority and dominion over the earth have been restored by the use of Yeshua's name. He has given mankind authority over the earth and also over the evil one and his demons. The Hebrew prophets—Yeshua, John, and Paul all said that Satan is the god of this world. We have been blaming God for what Satan has done. Yeshua said that Satan came only to steal, kill, and destroy (John 10:10). So, the rightful conclusion is that Satan caused the Holocaust. Hitler became a Satan-worshipper and was Satan's instrument to try to destroy ADONAI's first covenant people, Israel. The Messiah has been reaching out to the Jewish people for over 2000 years. God answers prayers in Yeshua's name. ADONAI offers us a fresh law—the law of the Spirit of life in Messiah Yeshua, which takes us out from under the law of sin and death. Yeshua is the new mediator between God and the human race: He has taken the place of the priests and He is the new High Priest. He hasn't forgotten you. You are the apple of His eye (Zechariah 2:8). God says,

> **Can a woman forget her nursing baby or lack compassion for a child of her womb? Even if these forget, I will not forget you. Behold, I have engraved you on the palms of My hands. — Isaiah 49:15–16**

You are His beloved. He paid the ultimate price for you at Golgotha. He has also passed great responsibility on to His followers. Yeshua, in His own synagogue, one Sabbath read the Scripture assigned to that day, which happened to be Isaiah 61, and He proclaimed it as personal to Himself. His ministry was to

> **bind up the broken-hearted, to proclaim liberty to the captives, and the opening of the prison to those who are bound, to proclaim the year of ADONAI's favor.** — Isaiah 61:1–2

Yeshua has passed this work on to His followers, but unfortunately many don't obey Him. Many followers of Yeshua during the Holocaust turned a blind eye to your suffering: some were even perpetrators. Please forgive us. Please forgive us. Forgive us our inhumanity and refusal to recognize that you are His beloved, His elect, and that He cherished you more than His own life. Forgive us. Yeshua is coming back soon. I long for you to know Him and His love for you.

MATHEMATICAL PATTERNS AND HIDDEN CODES IN SCRIPTURE

God has revealed Himself not only through the Hebrew Scriptures, but also through the four gospels, Matthew, Mark, Luke, and John, and the letters of Peter, John, Paul, James, and Jude, who were all Jewish. There is mathematical proof of the veracity of these Scriptures, just as there is of the Tanakh.

The importance of the number seven is underscored in both the Tanakh and the New Testament. The Sabbath is the seventh day of the week. On the seventh time that the Hebrews marched around Jericho, the city walls fell. The seventh year in Hebrew ancient law is *Shemitah*, when debts are cancelled. It took seven years to build the Temple in Jerusalem. In the book of Revelation, there are seven churches, seven seals, seven trumpets, seven spirits, and so on. So, the number seven is vitally important in God's dealings with us. Looking at Genesis 1 and Matthew 1, the first book of Jewish Scripture and the first book of the New Testament respectively, we also see the importance of seven. "In the beginning God created the heavens and the earth" contains seven Hebrew words. "In the beginning God created" has 14 letters (7×2). "The heavens and the earth" has 14 letters (7×2). The Hebrew letters of "God" + "heavens" + "earth" are 14 (7×2). Matthew 1:1-11 contains the first part of the genealogy of Jeshua. It contains 49 (7×7) vocabulary words (words without repetitions). The number of Hebrew letters in the 49 words is 266 (7×38).

Michael Dov Weissmandl found numerical patterns in the Torah. He found the first letter of a particularly significant word or phrase in a text and then counted a set number of letters to the next letter of the word or phrase, and then counted the same number of letters again to the third letter of the word or phrase and found meaningful words hidden in the text of the Torah. He found that the words occurred at equally spaced intervals, or ELS. His discoveries inspired research on ELS at the Hebrew University in the 1990s, done with the aid of computer programs. Yacov Rambsel used ELS to analyse the text of Isaiah 52, 53, and 54, which describe the suffering, death, burial, and resurrection of the Messiah. Jeshua, as well as many of the key figures around Jeshua at the time of His crucifixion are encoded in these messianic chapters. *Jeshua Shmi*, which means "Jeshua is my name," is encoded in Isaiah 53:10. The names of the High

Priests, Caiaphas and Annas, implicated in the death of Jeshua, are encoded in Isaiah 52 and 53. The names of all the disciples are encoded in Isaiah 53. Mary (there were three Marys at Jeshua's death including His mother) is encoded multiple times in these chapters. Jeshua was from Nazareth in Galilee, both of which are encoded in Isaiah 53. Caesar, who ruled over Israel at that time, is also encoded. The probability of these patterns of numbers in the Scriptures being made by humans is infinitely small and virtually impossible. These Bibles were written across 1600 years by 33 different people ranging from goat herders and uneducated fishermen to military generals and kings. They are no doubt what they propose to be—messages from God to us.

THANK YOU

I can't imagine what you have suffered. Bad things have happened to me, but they pale into insignificance compared to the horror you have experienced. But like you, I often ask God, "Why?" He tells me that some things I won't understand until the next life. In heaven we will be given answers.

But for now, it's war: war against a very powerful mastermind. We have to fight with all we have to gain protection, salvation, healing, and joy for ourselves and our loved ones. Although Satan robbed humanity of its power during the Fall, Yeshua has restored our dominion through belief in Him. This includes dominion over evil. We need to fight with Yeshua and in His authority: His name. God remembers you. He remembers His own.

I want to thank you for all you have given me. You gave me love and hope. You showed me God's face and demonstrated that love and courage win over evil in the end. You showed me the power of forgiveness. The Nazis and their evil god didn't destroy you or your race. They failed, and you are proof of this. Evil will never destroy Israel because you are the apple of His eye. And there will be an end to all this evil. The end is foretold in the book of Revelation and in the prophet Joel. Joel said that all nations will gather in the valley of Jehoshaphat and the sun and moon will become dark and heaven and earth will shudder. Revelation says that there will be a new heaven and a new earth. There will be justice.

> But *ADONAI* will be a refuge for His people, and a safe place for the children of Israel. — Joel 4:16

Part 4

Messianic Prophecies in Scripture

The Book of Matthew

*T*HERE IS A STRIKING resemblance between many of the prophecies in the Tanakh and the life, death, and ancestry of *Yeshua ha-Mashiach, Ben-David* as documented in the writings of Matthew, Mark, Luke, and John. Yeshua was born in Bethlehem during the reign of Herod, a king of Judea. At this time, when Caesar Augustus was emperor, the people of Judea were subject to Roman rule. Yeshua variously lived in Egypt, Nazareth, and Galilee and travelled around the Jewish towns and cities proclaiming that the kingdom of God had come. For most of Yeshua's life, Judea was ruled by Roman prefects. One of these prefects, Pontius Pilate, put Yeshua to death by crucifixion when He was thirty-three years old. The kohanim and scribes stirred the Jewish people to agitate for His execution, accusing Him of blasphemy. In the this part of the book, we draw out some of the similarities between the prophecies of the Messiah in the Tanakh and Yeshua Ben-David as portrayed in the gospels of Matthew, Mark, Luke, and John. There is much overlap between the four gospels, so we have concentrated on the similarities between the prophecies of the Messiah in the Tanakh and the life of Yeshua as portrayed in Matthew. We have only referred to the other three gospels when a point of similarity to the Tanakh is very pronounced.

Matthew was one of Yeshua's original twelve disciples and was an eyewitness to Yeshua's life. He recounts Yeshua's genealogy through Yeshua's step-father, Joseph, and gives details of His birth, life, and death.

Yeshua Descended from Abraham, Isaac, Jacob, and Judah

The book of the genealogy of *Yeshua ha-Mashiach, Ben-David, Ben-Avraham*: **Abraham fathered Isaac, Isaac fathered Jacob, Jacob fathered Judah and his brothers.** — Matthew 1:1–2

The first chapter of Matthew contains Yeshua's genealogy. Looking at the first chapter of Matthew, verses one and two correspond with Scriptures from Genesis and Numbers. They specifically correspond with Genesis 17:7 that the Messianic line would be through Abraham; Genesis 21:12 that Isaac would be the Messiah's ancestor; Genesis 28:14 and Numbers 24:17 that He would descend from Jacob; and Genesis 49:10 that the ruler would come from Judah. For the lineage of Yeshua, see also Luke 3:23–38.

Yeshua Descended from Jesse and King David

Jesse fathered David the king. David fathered Solomon by the wife of Uriah. — Matthew 1:6

Jesse is in Yeshua's lineage as seen in Matthew 1:5 and prophesied by Isaiah in chapter 11:1–2. King David was also a predecessor of Yeshua, as seen in this verse. Samuel prophesied in 2 Samuel 7:12–13 that the Messiah would come through David. Isaiah also saw this, as documented in chapter 9:7. See also 1 Chronicles 17:11.

Yeshua Was Divinely Conceived and the Offspring of a Virgin

Now the birth of Jeshua the Messiah happened in this way. When His mother Miriam was engaged to Joseph but before they came together, she was found to be pregnant through the *Ruach ha-Kodesh*. And Joseph her husband, being a righteous man and not wanting to disgrace her publicly, made up his mind to dismiss her secretly. But while he considered these things, behold an angel of ADONAI appeared to him in a dream, saying, "Joseph son of David, do not be afraid to take Miriam as your wife, for the Child conceived in her is from the *Ruach ha-Kodesh*. She will give birth to a son; and you shall call His name Yeshua, for He will save His people from their sins." Now all this took place to fulfill what was spoken by ADONAI through the prophet, saying, "Behold, the virgin shall conceive and give birth to a son, and they shall call His name Immanuel," which means "God with us."
— Matthew 1:18–23

The birth of Yeshua was miraculous as described in this passage from Matthew. The child was without a human father, being conceived by God Himself and prophesied by Isaiah in chapter

7:14 that a virgin would give birth. This text also resounds with Genesis 3:15 that the Messiah would be the seed of a woman. See also Luke 1:26–38.

Yeshua Was Born in Bethlehem

Now after Yeshua was born in Bethlehem of Judea, in the days of King Herod, magi from the east came to Jerusalem. — Matthew 2:1

Yeshua was born in Bethlehem, as seen from this verse. The prophet Micah in chapter 5:1–4 prophesied that the Messiah would be born in Bethlehem. See also Luke 2:4–7.

Yeshua Was Taken to Egypt

Now when they had gone, behold, an angel of ADONAI appears to Joseph in a dream, saying, "Get up! Take the Child and His mother and flee to Egypt. Stay there until I tell you, for Herod is about to search for the Child, to kill Him." So he got up, took the Child and His mother during the night, and went to Egypt. He stayed there until Herod's death. This was to fulfill what was spoken by ADONAI through the prophet, saying, "Out of Egypt I called My Son." Then when Herod saw that he had been tricked by the magi, he became furious. And he sent and killed all boys in Bethlehem and in all its surrounding area, from two years old and under, according to the time he had determined from the magi. — Matthew 2:13–16

In this passage from Matthew, we see that Yeshua was taken to Egypt to flee the evil King Herod, who had all the baby boys in Bethlehem killed. Hosea (11:1) prophesied that the Messiah would live in Egypt, and Jeremiah (31:14) saw a slaughter of young children.

Yeshua Grew Up in Natzeret

But when Herod died, behold, an angel of ADONAI appears in a dream to Joseph in Egypt, saying, "Get up! Take the Child and His mother and go to the land of Israel, for those seeking the Child's life are dead." So he got up, took the Child and His mother, and went to the land of Israel. But hearing that Archelaus was king of Judea in place of his father Herod, he became afraid to go there. Then after being warned in a dream, he withdrew to the region of the Galilee. And he went and lived in a city called Natzeret, to fulfill what was spoken through the prophets, that Yeshua shall be called a Natzrati. — Matthew 2:19–23

These verses from Matthew show that Yeshua was taken back to Israel from Egypt after Herod died, corresponding with Hosea's (11:1–2) prophecy that God's Son would be called out of Egypt. Joseph took Yeshua and Miriam to dwell in Nazareth, corresponding with Isaiah's (11:1–2) reference to the Messiah as "the Branch" or *neh-tzer*, which can be translated as Nazrati or Nazarene. Jeremiah (23:5) and Zechariah (6:12–13) also called the Messiah "the Branch."

A Messenger Went before Yeshua

In those days, John the Immerser came proclaiming in the wilderness of Judea, "Turn away from your

sins, for the kingdom of heaven is near!"
— Matthew 3:1–3

John the Baptiser went before Yeshua warning people to become holy, corresponding with Malachi's (3:11) prophecy that a messenger would go before the Messiah. See also John 1:23.

Yeshua Is God's Son

And behold, a voice from the heavens said, "This is My Son, whom I love; with Him I am well pleased!"
— Matthew 3:17

John baptized Yeshua in the Jordan river. As He came up out of the water, God could be heard calling Yeshua His Son, which corresponds with Psalm 2:7, where the Messiah is revealed as God's Son (Mark 1:9–11).

Yeshua Lived in Galilee

Now when Yeshua heard that John had been handed over, He withdrew to Galilee. Leaving Natzeret, He came and settled in Capernaum, which is by the sea in the regions of Zebulun and Naphtali.
— Matthew 4:12–13

Yeshua left Nazareth and went to live in Galilee, which concords with Isaiah 8:23–24, that the Messiah would be a Galilean.

Yeshua Was Mighty in the Ruach ha-Kodesh

News about Him spread throughout all Syria. And they brought to Him all the sick—those tormented by various diseases and afflictions, those plagued by

demons, the epileptics, the paralyzed—and He healed them. — Matthew 4:24

Yeshua set people free from afflictions. He proclaimed that the kingdom of heaven had come, and this was accompanied by many miracles. Isaiah, in chapter 35, saw that when salvation came to the Jewish people, many miracles would follow, and in chapter 61, Isaiah prophesied that the Messiah would be mighty in the Ruach ha-Kodesh and set the captives free.

Yeshua Reached Out to the Poor and the Meek

Now when Yeshua saw the crowds, He went up on the mountain. And after He sat down, His disciples came to Him. And He opened His mouth and began to teach them saying, "Blessed are the poor in spirit, for theirs is the kingdom of heaven. Blessed are those who mourn, for they shall be comforted. Blessed are the meek, for they shall inherit the earth. Blessed are those who hunger and thirst for righteousness, for they shall be satisfied. Blessed are the merciful, for they shall be shown mercy. Blessed are the pure in heart, for they shall see God. Blessed are the peacemakers, for they shall be called sons of God. Blessed are those who have been persecuted for the sake of righteousness, for theirs is the kingdom of heaven." — Matthew 5:1–10

Yeshua blessed the poor, the meek, and those who mourn, reflecting Isaiah in chapters 40:10–11 and 42:1–3, where he foresaw that the Messiah was sympathetic and compassionate.

Yeshua Healed All That Were Sick

> When evening came, the people brought to Him
> many who were afflicted by demons. He forced out
> the spirits with a word and healed all who were sick.
> So was fulfilled what was spoken through Isaiah the
> prophet, "He Himself took our sicknesses and carried
> away our diseases." — Matthew 8:16–17

Yeshua healed all that were sick. Isaiah, in chapters 35 and 61, prophesied that the Messiah would be a healer and deliverer.

Yeshua Performs Miracles

> Just as He was saying these things to them, a
> synagogue leader came and began to bow before
> Him, saying "My daughter has just died, but come lay
> Your hand on her and she will live." And Yeshua got
> up and began to follow him, with His disciples. Just
> then a woman, losing blood for twelve years, came
> from behind and touched the tzitzit of His garment.
> For she kept saying to herself, "If only I touch His
> garment, I will be healed." But then Yeshua turned
> and saw her. "Take heart, daughter," He said, "your
> faith has made you well." That very hour the woman
> was healed. When Yeshua came into the synagogue
> leader's house and saw the flute players and the noisy
> crowd wailing, He said, "Go away, for the girl isn't
> dead, but sleeping." And they began jeering at Him.
> But when the crowd had been cleared out, He went in
> and took her hand, and the girl got up.
> — Matthew 9:18–25

This passage describes the healing of a woman and of a girl being raised to life from death, which are a witness to the mighty power of God operating through Jeshua, corroborating Isaiah's prophecy in chapter 61, that the Ruach ha-Kodesh would be mighty in the Messiah.

Yeshua Is a Tender Shepherd

When He saw the crowds, He felt compassion for them, because they were harassed and helpless, like sheep without a shepherd. — Matthew 9:36

Isaiah 40:10 corresponds with this passage from Matthew in that Isaiah saw the Messiah as a tender shepherd.

Yeshua Healed the Sick

Knowing this, Yeshua went away from there, And large crowds followed Him, and He healed them all. — Matthew 12:15

Jeshua healed all that were sick. This echoes the 35th chapter of Isaiah where Isaiah prophesied that the lame would walk and the deaf would hear when Messiah comes.

Yeshua Speaks in Parables

In Matthew chapters 13, 20, 21, and 25, Yeshua speaks in parables, echoing Psalm 78:2, which suggests that the Messiah would communicate in parables.

Yeshua Has Compassion

**As Yeshua came ashore, He saw a large crowd and felt
compassion for them and healed their sick.
— Matthew 14:14**

In Isaiah 40:10–11, the prophet portrays the Messiah as a tender
and compassionate shepherd, reflected in this passage. It also
corresponds to Isaiah 35:2–6 where Isaiah sees that when the
Messiah comes there will be many wonderful miracles of God.

Yeshua Is God's Son

**While He was still speaking, suddenly a bright cloud
overshadowed them; and behold, a voice from out of
the cloud, saying, "This is My Son, whom I love; with
Him I am well pleased. Listen to Him!"
— Matthew 17:5**

This passage from Matthew also resonates with Psalm 2:7 where
God calls the Messiah His Son.

Yeshua Rides a Donkey's Colt into Jerusalem

**Now as they drew near to Jerusalem and came to
Bethphage, to the Mount of Olives, then Yeshua sent
two disciples, saying to them, "Go into the village
before you. Right away, you'll find a donkey tied up
and a colt with her. Untie them and bring them to
Me. If anyone says anything to you, you shall say,
'The Master needs them.' And right away he will send
them." — Matthew 21:1–3**

Yeshua entered Jerusalem riding on a donkey's colt, foretold by Zechariah in chapter 9:9 that Jerusalem would shout because its king was coming riding on the foal of a donkey. See also Luke 19:30–38 and Mark 11:1–11.

Infants Praise Yeshua

But when the ruling *kohanim* and *Torah* scholars saw the wonders He performed, and the children crying out in the Temple and saying, "*Hoshia-na* to Ben-David," they became indignant. — Matthew 21:15

In these verses, children praise Yeshua, echoing Psalm 8:3 that power is established through the very young. These verses indicate that Yeshua was in the Temple when it was still standing. It was prophesied by Malachi (3:1) that the Messiah would come to His Temple. Thus, the second Temple had to be standing at Messiah's coming. Similarly, Zechariah (11:13) prophesied that Messiah would come before the destruction of the Temple, as the thirty pieces of silver for which he was bought would be cast to the potter in the Temple.

Yeshua Is a Stumbling Block to Israel

Therefore I say to you, the kingdom of God will be taken away from you and given to people producing its fruits. Whoever falls on this stone will be shattered; but the one upon whom it falls, it will crush him. — Matthew 21:43–44

In these verses from Matthew, the Messiah will bring destruction to many Jewish people, reflecting Isaiah 8:14 that the Messiah will be a stumbling block to Israel.

Yeshua Was Betrayed by a Friend
for Thirty Pieces of Silver

**Then one of the Twelve, the one called Judah of Kriot,
went to the ruling kohanim and said, "What are you
willing to give me if I hand Him over to you?" And
they weighed out thirty shekels of silver for him.
From then on, Judah began looking for a chance to
hand Him over. — Matthew 26:14–15**

Yeshua was betrayed by Judah of Kriot, one of His followers,
foretold in Psalm 41:10, where King David saw that the Messiah
would be betrayed by His friend. Judah was given thirty pieces
of silver for handing Yeshua over to the kohanim, corresponding
with Zechariah's prophecy in 11:12 that the Messiah would be
valued at thirty pieces of silver. See also Mark 14:18, Luke 22:22,
and John 13:18.

Yeshua Was Arrested and His Disciples Were Scattered

**After singing the Hallel they went out to the Mount
of Olives. Then Yeshua said to them, "This night you
will all fall away because of Me; for it is written, 'I will
strike the Shepherd, and the sheep of the flock will be
scattered.'" — Matthew 26:30–31**

Yeshua and his followers gathered at the Mount of Olives after
the betrayal and Yeshua told His followers that they would all
desert Him. This corresponds to Zechariah's prophecy in 13:7
that the Shepherd would be struck and His sheep scattered.

Yeshua Is Humiliated

"Guilty," they answered. "He deserves death!" Then
they spat on His face and pounded Him with their
fists. Others slapped Him and demanded, "Prophesy
to us, you Messiah! Which one hit You?"
— Matthew 26:66–68

At Yeshua's trial by the kohen gadol, when all the kohanim and
sanhedrin were gathered, the kohanim gadol accused Yeshua
of blasphemy and the crowd gave their verdict of "Guilty." This
passage resonates with Isaiah 50:6 that the Messiah did not hide
His face from humiliation and spitting.

The Thirty Pieces of Silver Are Given to Buy a Potter's Field

Then Judah His betrayer, saw that Yeshua had been
condemned. Feeling remorse, he brought the thirty
silver pieces back to the ruling kohanim and elders,
saying, "I've sinned, betraying innocent blood!" But
they said "What's that to us? You see to it yourself!"
After tossing the silver into the Temple sanctuary, he
left. Then he went off and hanged himself. But the
ruling kohanim took the silver pieces and said, "It
is not permitted to put these in the treasury, since
it is blood money." So after they conferred, they
bought with them the potter's field, as a cemetery for
strangers. For this reason that field has been called
the "Field of Blood" to this day. — Matthew 27:3–8

Zechariah (11:12) wrote that the thirty pieces of silver paid for
the Messiah would be thrown to the potter. In this passage from

Matthew, Judah felt great remorse for what he had done and tossed the coins in the Temple and killed himself. The kohanim bought the potter's field with the money, thus fulfilling prophecy.

Yeshua Has Many Enemies

> Now the ruling kohanim and elders persuaded the crowds that they should ask for Bar-Abba and destroy Yeshua. But the governer responded, "Which of the two do you want me to release for you?" And they said "Bar-Abba!" Pilate said to them, "What then shall I do with Yeshua, who is called Messiah?" "Execute Him!" all of them say. — Matthew 27:20–22

These verses describe the hatred of the crowds for Yeshua, inspired by the kohanim, reflecting Psalm 69:5 that the Messiah's enemies would be more than can be counted.

Yeshua Is Humiliated and Tortured

> Then the governor's soldiers took Jeshua into the Praetorium and gathered the whole cohort around Him. They stripped Him and put a scarlet robe around Him. And after braiding a crown of thorns, they placed it on His head and put a staff in His right hand. And falling on their knees before Him, they mocked Him, saying, "Hail, King of the Jews!" They spat on Him, and they took the staff and beat Him over and over on the head. — Matthew 27:27–30

As did the previous passage in Matthew 26:67, these verses resemble Isaiah 50:6 where the Messiah is tortured and humiliated. See also Mark 15:16–20.

Yeshua Is Given Gall and Vinegar, and His Clothes Are Gambled For

They offered Him wine mixed with gall to drink; but after tasting, He was unwilling to drink it. And when they had crucified Him, they divided His clothing among themselves by casting lots.
— Matthew 27:34–35

Yeshua was beaten, tortured, humiliated, and hung on a tree with two others. He was given gall mixed with wine to drink. In Psalm 69 (21–22), David foresaw that the Messiah would be given gall and vinegar in His great suffering. In Psalm 22:19, David predicted that the Messiah's clothes would be gambled for. In Genesis 3:15, the Messiah's heel would be bruised by the devil. See also Mark 15:36.

Yeshua Is Taunted

"He trusts in God; let God rescue Him now if He wants Him." — Matthew 27:43

Yeshua's executioners taunted Him because He trusted in God but God did not rescue Him from death, reflecting David's verse in Psalm 22:9.

Yeshua Is Abandoned by ADONAI

About the ninth hour Yeshua cried out with a loud voice, saying, *"Eli, Eli, lema sabachthani?"*
— Matthew 27:45–46

Yeshua uttered the opening words from Psalm 22—"My God, My God, why have You forsaken Me?" at the point of death.

Yeshua Is Buried with the Rich

Now when it was evening, there came a rich man
from Arimathea, named Joseph, who had also
become a disciple of Yeshua. This man went to Pilate
and asked for Yeshua's body. Then Pilate ordered it to
be given up. And Joseph took the body and wrapped
it in a clean linen cloth. And he laid it in his own new
tomb, which he had cut in the rock.
— Matthew 27:57–60

After Yeshua's death, Joseph, a disciple of his who was a rich man, buried Yeshua in his tomb, which corresponds with Isaiah 53:9, where the prophet sees that the Messiah would be buried with the rich. See also Mark 15:42–46.

Yeshua Rises from the Dead

"He is not here; for He has risen, just as He said."
— Matthew 28:6

After Yeshua's death and burial, an angel appeared to some of His women disciples saying that He had risen from the dead. This corresponds with Isaiah's prophecy in 53:12 that the Messiah would be killed but be greatly rewarded and thus live again. It was also foretold in Psalm 16:10 that the Messiah's body would not suffer corruption nor His soul stay in the place of the dead. See also Mark 16, Luke 24, and John 20.

The Book of Mark

*M*ARK WROTE THE DISCIPLE Peter's teachings and became an evangelist with Barnabas, as documented in the book of Acts.

Yeshua Establishes a New Covenant

And while they were eating, He took matzah; and after He offered the bracha, He broke it and gave it to them and said, "Take; this is My body." And He took a cup; and after giving thanks, He gave to them and they all drank from it. And He said to them, "This is My blood of the covenant, which is poured out for many." — Mark 14:22–24

Before Yeshua was arrested, He celebrated Passover in Jerusalem with His followers. He said that the matzah was His body and that His blood was covenant blood poured out for many. He intimates that He is the Passover Lamb whose sacrifice was for the people's sins. He foretells that in His death a new covenant will be forged with the Jewish people and perhaps with the whole human race. In chapter 31, Jeremiah talked of a new covenant, which would be made with Israel: a covenant that would be written in people's hearts. See also Luke 22:20.

Yeshua Is Humiliated and Tortured

> **The soldiers took Him away, into the palace, the governer's mansion called the Praetorium. And they call together the cohort of soldiers. They dress Him up in purple. After braiding a crown of thorns, they put it on Him. And they began to salute Him, "Hail, King of the Jews!" Over and over, they kept hitting Him on the head with a staff and spitting on Him; and kneeling down, they worshipped Him. When they finished mocking Him, they stripped the purple off Him and put His own clothes back on Him. And they led Him out to crucify Him.**
> **— Mark 15:16–20**

Before Yeshua was executed, He was ridiculed, spat upon, and tortured, reminiscent of Isaiah's words in 50:6 that the Messiah gave His body to torture and humiliation.

Yeshua Is Seated at the Right Hand of God

> **Then the Lord Yeshua, after He had spoken to them, was taken up into heaven and sat down at the right hand of God. — Mark 16:19**

Psalm 110:1 declares that the Messiah will be seated at the right hand of God. In these verses from Mark, Yeshua, after rising from the dead, ascends to the right hand of the Almighty in heaven.

Chapter 8

The Book of Luke

LUKE WAS A PHYSICIAN who accompanied Paul, as mentioned in Paul's writings to Philemon. Luke's genealogy of Yeshua's ancestry is through Mary, His mother.

Yeshua Is a Light in the Darkness

Through our God's heart of mercy, the Sunrise from on high will come upon us, to give light to those who sit in darkness and in the shadow of death, to guide our feet in the way of shalom. — Luke 1:78–79

As seen in Isaiah 9:1–2, Jeshua came as a light to those in darkness and under death's shadow and power.

Yeshua Is Born During Caesar Augustus' Reign

Now it happened in those days a decree went out from Caesar Augustus to register all the world's inhabitants. — Luke 2:1

This verse places the date of Yeshua's birth during the reign of Caesar Augustus, which is concordant with Daniel's (9:26) prophecy that the Messiah would come before the destruction of the Temple and Jerusalem in 70 AD.

Yeshua Is a Light to the Nations

A light for revelation to the nations. — Luke 2:32

In Isaiah 9:1–2 and 49:6–7, the Messiah will be a light and salvation not just to the Jewish people but to all nations, as is echoed in this verse by Luke.

Yeshua Descends from Shem, Jacob, Judah, Jesse, and David

The son of David, the son of Jesse, the son of Obed, the son of Boaz, the son of Salmon, the son of Nahshon, the son of Amminadab, the son of Ram, the son of Hezron, the son of Perez, the son of Judah, the son of Jacob, the son of Yitzhak, the son of Abraham, the son of Terah, the son of Nahor, the son of Serug, the son of Reu, the son of Peleg, the son of Eber, the son of Shelah, the son of Cainan, the son of Arphaxad, the son of Shem, the son of Noah, the son of Lamech, the son of Methuselah, the son of Enoch, the son of Jared, the son of Mahalalel, the son of Kenan, the son of Enosh, the son of Seth, the son of Adam, the son of God. — Luke 3:31–38

This passage from Luke contains a more comprehensive genealogy than the first chapter of Matthew. It is in line with Genesis 9:26 that the Messiah would descend from Shem; Numbers 24:17 that He would descend from Jacob; Psalm 78:67 that the Messiah would descend from Judah; Isaiah 11:1–2 that He would descend from Jesse; and 2 Samuel 7:12 and Isaiah 9:5 that He would descend from David.

Yeshua Fulfills Isaiah 61

"The *Ruach of* ADONAI is on me, because He has
anointed me to proclaim Good News to the poor.
He has sent me to proclaim release to the captives
and recovery of sight to the blind, to set free the
oppressed, and to proclaim the year of ADONAI's
favor." He closed the scroll, gave it back to the
attendant, and sat down. . . . "Today this Scripture
has been fulfilled in your ears." — Luke 4:18–21

In this passage from Luke, Yeshua actually declares that Isaiah
61 is being fulfilled by Himself.

Yeshua Is Mighty in the Ruach ha-Kodesh

Just as he came near the town gate, behold, a dead
man was being carried out, the only son of his
mother, a widow. A considerable crowd from the
town was with her. When the Lord saw her, He felt
compassion for her and said, "Don't cry." Then He
came up and touched the coffin, and the pallbearers
came to a standstill. He said, "Young man! I tell you,
get up!" The dead man sat up and began speaking,
and Yeshua gave him to his mother. — Luke 7:12–15

Yeshua raised a young man from death just as He raised a young
girl from death (as documented in Matthew 9:18). This corresponds to Isaiah's proclamation in chapters 35 and 61 that the
Ruach of God would be mighty in the Messiah performing miracles of healing and deliverance.

Yeshua Sets a Captive Free

They sailed over to the country of the Gerasenes,
which is on the opposite side of the Galilee. A demon-
plagued man from the town met Yeshua as He was
coming out onto the land. The man hadn't worn any
clothing for a long time and was living not in a house
but in the tombs. Seeing Yeshua, he cried out and
fell down before Yeshua, and with a loud voice said
"What's between You and me, Yeshua, Ben-El Eyon?
I'm begging You, do not torment me!" For Yeshua
commanded the defiling spirit to come out of the
man. For many times it had seized him so that, even
though he was restrained and bound with chains and
shackles, he would break the chains and be driven by
the demons into the desert. Yeshua questioned him,
"What is your name?" "Legion," he said, for many
demons had entered him. They kept begging Him
not to command them to depart into the abyss. Now
a large herd of pigs was feeding on the mountain.
The demons urged Yeshua to let them enter these
pigs, and He gave them permission. Then the demons
came out of the man and entered into the pigs. The
herd rushed down the cliff into the lake and was
drowned. — Luke 8:26–33

Yeshua not only healed the sick and raised the dead, but as seen
in this verse, He delivered people from demonic possession, in
line with Isaiah's prophecy in chapter 61 that the Messiah would
set the captives free.

Yeshua Sees Satan Falling from Heaven

And Yeshua said to them, "I was watching satan fall like lightning from heaven. Behold, I have given you authority to trample upon serpents and scorpions, and over all the power of the enemy; nothing will harm you." — Luke 10:18–19

In this passage, Yeshua sees the fall of Satan prophesied in Genesis 3:15, that the devil would be crushed by the Messiah.

Yeshua Establishes a New Covenant in His Blood

"This cup is the new covenant in My blood, which is poured out for you." — Luke 22:20

In this passage from Luke, Yeshua actually states that the new covenant is in His blood shed for us. This new covenant was foretold by Jeremiah in chapter 31:30.

Yeshua Was Counted with Transgressors

Others, two evildoers, were also led away to be put to death with Him. When they came to the place called the Skull, there they crucified Him and the evildoers, one on His right and the other on His left. — Luke 23:32

Yeshua was executed with two criminals, one on His right and one on His left, corresponding with Isaiah 53:12, which foretells that the Messiah would be counted with the transgressors.

Yeshua's Clothing Is Gambled For

Then they cast lots, dividing up the clothing.
— Luke 23:34

After His execution, Yeshua's clothes were gambled for, which was foreseen by David in Psalm 22:19.

Chapter 9

The Book of John

OHN WAS ONE OF Yeshua's twelve disciples and he claims the gospel of John is an eyewitness account.

Yeshua Is the Light of Humanity

In Him was life, and the life was the light of men. The light shines in the darkness, and the darkness has not overpowered it. — John 1:4–5

This passage resonates with Isaiah 9:1–2, that the Messiah will bring great light. In these verses, Yeshua is referred to as the light of mankind.

Yeshua Was Rejected by His Own People

He came to His own, but His own did not receive Him. — John 1:11

Isaiah foresaw that the Messiah would be rejected and not believed by His own people in Isaiah chapter 53:1. Yeshua was rejected by the majority of Jews.

Yeshua Is the Lamb of God

The next day, John sees Yeshua coming to him and says, "Behold, the Lamb of God who takes away the sin of the world!" — John 1:29

In this text, John the Immerser proclaims that Yeshua is the Lamb of God, which resonates with Isaiah 53 where the Messiah is likened to a sheep led to the slaughter and that, as did the Passover lamb, He would bear people's sins.

Jeshua Is Mighty in the Ruach ha-Kodesh

"The One who sent me to immerse in water said to me, 'The One on whom you see the *Ruach* coming down and remaining, this is the One who immerses in *Ruach ha-Kodesh.*'" — John 1:33

John the Immerser declares that Yeshua baptizes in the Holy Spirit. This is in line with Isaiah 61 that the Messiah is mighty in the Ruach of God and Zechariah 12:10 that God would pour out His Spirit on the Jewish people.

Yeshua Is a Great Prophet

"This is most certainly the Prophet who is to come into the world!" — John 6:14

Yeshua fed a large crowd with only a few pieces of fish and a few loaves of bread. When the crowd saw what He had done, they said that He was the Prophet spoken of by Moses in Deuteronomy 18:15–18.

Yeshua Is the Good Shepherd

**"I am the Good Shepherd. The Good Shepherd lays
down His life for the sheep." — John 10:11**

In the words of Yeshua, He is the Good Shepherd who gives
His life for the sheep, echoing Isaiah 40: 10–11 that the Messiah
would be a loving and caring shepherd who gently cares for His
flock.

Yeshua Is Not Believed and Trusted

**But even though He had performed so many signs
before them, they weren't trusting in Him. This was
to fulfill the word of Isaiah the prophet, who said,
"ADONAI, who has believed our report? To whom has
the arm of ADONAI been revealed?" — John 12:37–38**

This Scripture also speaks of the unbelief of the Jewish people
toward Yeshua corresponding to the first verses of Isaiah 53.

Yeshua Is Betrayed

**"He who eats My bread has lifted up his heel against
Me." — John 13:18**

In this Scripture, Yeshua states that one of His followers would
betray Him, fulfilling Psalm 41:10.

Yeshua Is Scourged

**Then Pilate took Yeshua and had Him scourged.
— John 19:1**

Yeshua was scourged before His execution—Isaiah wrote in both 50:6 and 53:4 that the Messiah would be scourged.

Yeshua Is Crucified

Then they took Yeshua. He went out, carrying His own crossbar, to the Place of a Skull, which in Aramaic is called Golgotha. There they crucified Him, and with Him two others, one each side and Yeshua in between. — John 19:17–18

Yeshua was crucified. ADONAI said in Genesis 3:15 that the devil would bruise the Messiah's heel. See also Mark 15:23–24.

Yeshua's Bones Are Not Broken but His Side Is Pierced

So the soldiers came and broke the legs of the first and then the other who had been executed with Yeshua. Now when they came to Yeshua and saw that He was already dead, they did not break His legs. But one of the soldiers pierced His side with a spear, and immediately blood and water came out.
—John 19:32–34

At Yeshua's crucifixion, one of the Roman soldiers came to break His legs to kill Him, but realizing that He was already dead, he pierced His side. Corresponding to this, Zechariah 12:10 foretold that the Messiah would be pierced. King David in Psalm 22 envisioned that the Messiah would have His hands and feet pierced. When David wrote this, crucifixion was not familiar to Jewish people. Execution was by stoning. Crucifixion came in with Roman occupation. It was a very cruel way of killing a person and involved the victim's hands and feet being nailed to a piece of wood. However, like the Passover lamb in Exodus 12:46, used to protect the Israelites in Egypt, none of Yeshua's bones were broken. This was also prophesied in Psalm 34:21, that not a bone shall be broken.

Yeshua Ben-David from Nazareth Fulfills Tanakh Prophesies

In conclusion, it appears that specific details of the Messiah were recorded in the Tanakh from Genesis through Malachi, and these details paint a picture of the ancestry, conception, birth, birthplace, character, ministry, suffering, death, burial, and resurrection of Yeshua Ben-David from Nazareth.

All points of His ancestry match the prophecies in the Tanakh—that the Messiah would be a descendant of Noah, Shem, Abraham, Isaac, Jacob, Judah, Jesse, and David. Micah prophesied the Messiah would be born in Bethlehem, Isaiah that He would be a Nazarene and also a Galilean, and Hosea that He would come out of Egypt, all matching the life of Yeshua as recorded in the gospels. Isaiah prophesied that He would be a tender-hearted, compassionate leader, which was true of Yeshua. King David, Isaiah, and Zechariah all saw the Messiah suffering a cruel execution. The fine details of the execution were recorded, such as that He would be given vinegar to drink, that He would be pierced, that He would be killed along with criminals, and that His clothes would be gambled for. These details were all fulfilled in the death of Yeshua. Zechariah even prophesied that He would be bought for thirty pieces of silver and that the money would be cast to the potter, which are fulfilled in the betrayal of Yeshua by Judah of Kriot in the gospels. Isaiah saw that He would be buried with the rich; Yeshua was buried in the tomb of a rich man, Joseph of Arimathea.

Isaiah foretold that He would be a sacrifice for our sins and the prophet Jeremiah foretold that there would be a new covenant between God and humanity. The New Testament, or New Covenant of Yeshua, says that Yeshua is the Lamb of God who took our sins on Himself and that He is the fulfillment of Jewish law. Isaiah 46:9–10 reads, "For I am God—there is no other. I am God, and there is none like Me—declaring the end from the beginning, from ancient time what is to come, saying 'My purpose will stand, and I will accomplish all that I please.'"

Isaiah also foretold that the Messiah, although killed, would live, and King David prophesied that He would not be abandoned to Sheol or suffer corruption. There were many witnesses to Yeshua being alive after His execution and death, which points to the supernatural power of God. Yeshua asked His disciples, "But who do you say I am?" Peter answered, "You are the Messiah, the Son of the living God." Yeshua said to him, "Blessed are you, Simon, son of Jonah, because flesh and blood did not reveal this to you, but My Father who is in heaven!" (Matthew 16:15–17). Thus, Yeshua Himself said that He was God's Chosen One.

The prophet Daniel foresaw that the Messiah would come before the destruction of the Temple, as did Malachi and Zechariah. There are many passages in the gospels describing Yeshua in the second Temple.

The life of Yeshua Ben-David meets all the requirements of the Messiah spoken by prophets centuries before His birth.

Further, hidden codes in the Tanakh found using ELS also mark Yeshua as the coming Messiah and the same patterns of numbers found in the Tanakh are also found in the New Testament. We turn to these now.

Part 5

Hidden Codes and Numerical Patterns in Scripture

Chapter 10

Yeshua Is Encoded in the Tanakh

SURPRISINGLY, YACOV RAMBSEL (2000) found the name "Yeshua" encoded in Genesis. Take Genesis 3:15, "And I will put animosity between you and the woman—between your seed and her seed." Counting from the second word and the third letter backwards, every 69th letter reads "Yeshua." Letters next to these at the same distance read "atonement for all." Thus, ADONAI encoded the name of the seed of the woman who would bruise the head of the serpent—Yeshua—and that He would be an atonement. Take Genesis 3:12, "Then the man said, 'The woman you gave to be with me—she gave me of the Tree, and I ate.'" Take the 11th word and the third letter and count backwards 46 letters and you find "tzalab" or "crucify" or "cross." Letters next to these and encoded at the same distance spell "lamb." Similarly, take Exodus 12:29, "So it came about at midnight that ADONAI struck down all the firstborn in the land of Egypt, from the firstborn of Pharaoh sitting on his throne to the firstborn of the captive who was in the dungeon, and all the firstborn cattle." Counting backwards every 37th letter from the fourth word and third letter, reads "the cross" and letters next to these at the same distance spell "for Yeshua." Thus, the description of the first Passover has encoded in it the name of Yeshua, the Passover Lamb of God and His means of execution.

As seen earlier, Psalm 22, written by King David, gives a graphic description of the execution of the Messiah. Yeshua's name is encoded many times in the text of Psalm 22. Take Psalm 22:17, "For dogs have surrounded me. A band of evildoers has closed in on me. They pierced my hands and my feet." Counting backwards every 26th letter from the fifth word and third letter reads "the sign for Yeshua," which has a probability of 1 in 10^{10}. Psalm 22:13 reads, "Many bulls have surrounded me. Strong bulls of Bashan encircled me." Take the eighth word and the second letter and count backwards every 45th letter and it reads "Yeshua Mashiachi," or "Yeshua my Messiah." The probability of this is 1 in 10^{18}. The name of Yeshua is also encoded in Leviticus. Take Leviticus 21:10, "He who is the *kohen gadol* among his brothers, upon whose head the anointing oil is poured and is consecrated to put on the garments, is not to let the hair of his head hang loose or tear his clothes." Counting forwards every third letter from the first word and second letter we read, "Behold, the blood of Yeshua." Thus, a Scripture that talks about the High Priest who makes atonement by blood sacrifice of animals has encoded in it the name of Yeshua, who would pay the price for our sins through the shedding of His blood (Rambsel 2000).

The name of Yeshua is also encoded many times in the text of Isaiah, the Hebrew prophet living in the 8th century BC. Isaiah 53, 52, and 54 describe the suffering, death, burial, and resurrection of the Jewish Messiah. The name of Yeshua, as well as many of the key figures around Jesus at the time of His crucifixion, are all encoded in these Messianic chapters from Isaiah. *Yeshua Shmi* means "Yeshua is My name." It is encoded in Isaiah 53:10, which reads, "Yet it pleased ADONAI to bruise Him, He caused Him to suffer. If He makes His soul a guilt offering, He will see His offspring, He will prolong His days, and the will of ADONAI will succeed by His hand." Beginning with the second Hebrew letter, yod, in "he shall prolong," and counting every 20th letter from the left to the right reads, "Yeshua Shmi." "Yeshua is My strong name" is encoded in Isaiah 53:11 with a probability of 1 in 10^{12} (Rambsel 2000).

The name of Yeshua is similarly encoded in many other of the messianic passages in the Tanakh. For instance, the name Yeshua is encoded in Psalm 41:8–9, which speaks of the Messiah's betrayal; in Zechariah 11:12, which foretells the price paid for Yeshua by Judah of Kriot; in Zechariah 12:10, which talks of "the one whom they pierced"; and in Isaiah 61:1–2, which proclaims that the Ruach ha-Kodesh is upon the Messiah. And chapter 9 of the book of Daniel, which prophesies of the Messiah, has "Yeshua," "Nazarene," and "Branch" encoded (Jeffrey 1998).

Many significant people, places, and events in Yeshua's life and death are encoded in Isaiah 52 and 53. For example, the name Caiaphas, who was the high priest that organized the plot to kill Yeshua, is encoded in Isaiah 52. The name of another high priest, Annas, is encoded in Isaiah 53. All the names of the disciples are likewise encoded in the fifty-third chapter of Isaiah.

Yeshua was from Nazareth in Galilee. Both Nazarene and Galilee are encoded in Isaiah 53. Likewise, Caesar and Herod, the rulers over Israel at the time of Yeshua are encoded. The name Mary is encoded in Isaiah 53 multiple times. Around the same verses, the name John is also encoded. The gospel of John identified three Marys at Yeshua's death and also the disciple John. Rambsel (2000) says that there are hundreds of associations with Yeshua around the time of, and leading up to, His death encoded in Isaiah 53. (There is Bible code software available for download from the internet. For instance, from TES www.jewishsoftware.com and Bible Codes Plus.)

Numerical Patterns in New Covenant Scripture

*J*UST AS THE NUMBER seven occurs underneath the surface of the text of the Tanakh, it also occurs in the New Testament. Ivan Panin discovered amazing things by looking at patterns of sevens in the first chapter of Matthew. The first chapter of the New Testament contains Yeshua's genealogy, recorded in Matthew 1:1–17. Vocabulary words are the total number of words in a text without the repetitions. In these verses, there are 72 vocabulary words, and the gematria of these words added together is 42,364 (6052 × 7). There are 56 (8 × 7) nouns in the verses, and "the" occurs 56 (8 × 7) times. The genealogy contains two sections, the first being verses 1–11 and the second being verses 12–17. The number of vocabulary words in verses 1–11 is 49 (7 × 7). The number of letters in these 49 words is 266 (38 × 7). Of the 266 letters, there are 140 (20 × 7) vowels and 126 (18 × 7) consonants. Of the 49 vocabulary words, the number of words starting with vowels is 28 (7 × 4). The number of words starting with consonants is 21 (7 × 3). The number of nouns is 42 (7 × 6). Of these nouns, 35 (5 × 7) are proper names. There are 28 (4 × 7) male names, which occur 56 (8 × 7) times in the text. Three women's names are in this section with a total number of Greek letters of 14 (2 × 7). These are just a few of many instances where the number seven appears below the surface of the first chapter of Matthew. The second chapter of Matthew is similarly saturated with instances of the number seven occurring beneath the surface of the text. Panin uncovered many thousands of numerical features in the text of the New Testament. The chances of these features occurring together in passages by chance is astronomically small (Panin 1934; Sabiers 1941).

By looking at the gematria of words in the Greek texts, further astounding discoveries have been made. Both the Jews and the Greeks used alphabet letters to represent numbers, so in the English system the letter "A" would also be the number "one" in Hebrew and Greek. Each word has a numeric value found by totalling the numbers of the letters. In the same way, each sentence and paragraph also has a numeric value. This is the gematria of the letter, word, or passage. For example, Jesus in Greek is IESOUS. The gematria for I is 10, E is 8, S is 200, O is 17, U is 400, and S is 200. These numbers add up to 888. The gematria of Christ is 1480 (8 × 185). Saviour is 1408 (8 × 176). Lord is 800 (8 × 100). Messiah is 656 (8 × 82). The Son of Man is 2960 (8 × 370), and The Truth is 64 (8 × 8) (Stanton n.d.). Thus, Yeshua's number is 8.

Just as Yeshua has a number, the devil also has a number. Satan is variously called Dragon, Tempter, Belial, Murderer, and

Serpent. Satan is called dragon 13 times and the gematria of dragon is 975 (13 × 75). Tempter occurs 1053 (13 × 81) times. Belial occurs 78 (13 × 6) times. Murderer occurs 1820 (13 × 140) times. Serpent occurs 780 (13 × 60) times. The phrase in Revelation 12:9, "called the devil and Satan," has a gematria of 2197 (13 × 13 × 13). The New Testament says that God has made Christ sin for us although He knew no sin. The plaque above Yeshua's cross at Golgotha read "Jesus of Nazareth." The gematria of this is 2197 (13 × 13 × 13) (Stanton n.d.). On the cross, Yeshua said, "My God, My God, why have You forsaken Me?" He became sin because He bore our sin, and God turned His eyes from Yeshua.

Part 6

Conclusion

Chapter 12

In Summary

*T*HUS, IT IS EVIDENT that there is a new covenant between God and humankind, which was foretold by Jeremiah the prophet. The new covenant is first for the Jewish people and also made through blood sacrifice. We read in Leviticus that there is no forgiveness of sin without the shedding of blood (Leviticus 17:11). King David and the prophets Isaiah and Zechariah all foresaw a brutal execution. Isaiah prophesied that the man would be cruelly killed, but in dying, He would bear our sin and iniquity. He was led as a lamb to the slaughter. The text in Exodus 12:29, which describes the first Passover killing of a lamb, has the name of Yeshua encoded in it. In Leviticus 21:10, the name of Yeshua is encoded in a text about the kohen gadol who made the animal sacrifices in the Temple to atone for the sins of Israel. Likewise, the name of Yeshua is encoded in King David's and Isaiah's prophecies of the Messiah's execution. These are not coincidences, but God's way of saying to the Jewish people, and indeed to the people of the whole world, that Yeshua Ben-David is His Chosen One—the Passover Lamb whose blood was shed for our sins. Mark Biltz (2014) points out that Yeshua's death occurred at God's perfect timing. In Mark 15:25, we read that at the third hour (or 9 a.m.) they crucified Yeshua. So, when the Passover lamb was being prepared, at the same time Yeshua was being executed at Golgotha outside of Jerusalem. Matthew 27:45–46 reads that from the sixth hour (midday) until the ninth hour (3 p.m.), darkness was over the land: "About the ninth hour Yeshua cried out with a loud voice, saying, '*Eli, Eli, lema sabachthani?*' that is, 'My God, My God, why have You abandoned Me?'" The sacrifice of the lamb in the afternoon occurred at the ninth hour, the same time that Yeshua died. So, even the hour of Yeshua's death matched the time of Passover.

The animal sacrifices could not take place after the destruction of the Temple in 70 AD. So, it appeared that there was no forgiveness of sin any more. However, Daniel prophesied that the Messiah would come before the destruction of the Temple. This also points to the Messiah being Yeshua Ben-David and that He was, and is, the Lamb of God who takes away the sins of the world.

The encoding of significant names, places, and events in the Tanakh is proof that it is the handiwork of God. The encoding of Yeshua's name and the people and places associated with His life, death, and ministry in the Tanakh is further indication that He is God's Chosen. As the number seven running through the text of the Tanakh further highlights the divine authorship of the text, so the patterns of number in the gospels of Yeshua underscore the message of the gospels that the New Testament is a continuation of the Tanakh and Yeshua Ben-David is indeed the Jewish Messiah.

ADONAI established a new covenant through Yeshua. Leviticus 17:11 reads, "For the life of the creature is in the blood, and I have given it to you on the altar to make atonement for your lives—for it is the blood that makes atonement because of the life." Through shedding His blood, people's sins are forgiven and they enter into a new birth where their hearts are circumcised to love God and others. The law is written in their hearts as the prophet Jeremiah foresaw. It is actually God Himself who lives in our hearts at the new birth. Yeshua said, "If anyone loves Me, he will keep My word. My Father will love him, and We will come to him and make Our dwelling with him" (John 14:23). The new birth is activated by faith that Yeshua is God's Chosen and that His death on Golgotha paid the price for our sins so that we would have a new nature aligned to God's ways. We would have love in our hearts and a deep desire to obey His commandments. Right standing with God is not through keeping the law, but it is through relationship with ADONAI, who lives in our hearts and make us faithful to Him by His indwelling presence.

When Yeshua died at Golgotha, Matthew recorded that the curtain of the Temple was split in two from top to bottom (Matthew 27:51). The curtain, or veil, separated the Holy of Holies from the outer parts of the Temple. It was prophesied in 1 Kings 8:27 and Isaiah 66:1 that God cannot be contained in a house made by humans, and it was written in Acts 7:48 that, "However, Elyon does not dwell in man-made houses" and in 17:24 that "the God who made the world and all things in it, since He is Lord of heaven and earth, does not live in temples made by hands." The Jewish Temple no longer stands. No building can be said to contain God any more. But in the New Testament of Yeshua Ben-David, it is said a number of times that God makes His home with us and even *in* us. For instance, Ephesians 3:17 says, "So that Messiah may dwell in your hearts through faith"; Colossians 1:27 reads, "which is Messiah in you, the hope of glory"; Galatians 2:20 says, "and it is no longer I who live, but Messiah lives in me"; 1 Corinthians 6:19 reads, "Or don't you know that your body is a Temple of the *Ruach ha-Kodesh* who is in you." The Holy Place of God is actually us. We are God's Temple. God is Spirit. He made us in His likeness. We are spirit beings, but because Adam and Eve sinned, God had to take His presence out of their spirits. When the first man and woman obeyed Satan, he became their lord. The work of Yeshua is described in the New Covenant: Yeshua came to destroy the works of the devil (1 John 4:8). Yeshua bought us back from ownership by the devil, and He can come and live in our spirits as He did with Adam and Eve. What a glorious hope that your Messiah wants to live inside you—inside your human spirit through the work of redemption accomplished at Golgotha. Instead of going to the Temple to worship, God's original plan is now in action, namely that God can once again come and live in the human spirit of those born of the Ruach ha-Kodesh. This is the essence of God's plan presented first of all to the Jewish people and then to the Gentiles. Through God living in our hearts, we can be sure of eternity in heaven. We are also given the grace to rule in life. We can do all things through Him who strengthens us (Philippians 4:13); we can have what we say (Mark 11:23); and we can have what we ask in Yeshua's name (John 14:14). Yeshua has given His followers authority over all evil (Luke 10:18–20) as He has been given all authority in heaven and in earth (Matthew 28:18). Therefore, we have authority over sickness, poverty, and any evil that would come against us.

In Ephesians 2:14, Paul says that Yeshua has broken down the dividing wall between Jew and Gentile, abolishing in His flesh the hostility between them. He has created one new man from the two who were formerly separated. In the book of Romans, Paul says that the Gentiles are cut from a wild olive tree and grafted onto the cultivated olive tree, which is the Jewish people. He says, "How much more will these natural branches [the Jews] be grafted into their own olive tree?" (Romans 11:24). He writes in Romans 11:25–26 that when the fullness of the Gentiles comes "all Israel will be saved."

Chapter 13

How Do the Newly Discovered Facts Affect Us?

(**Excerpt from** *Mathematics Proves Holy Scriptures* **by Karl Sabiers,**
available from Amazon and www.NewEnglandBibleSales.com. Scripture
quotes in this excerpt are from the King James Bible.)

*W*E HAVE SEEN BEFORE our very eyes an actual sci-
entific demonstration of the divine verbal inspiration of
the Bible—a demonstration consisting of facts discovered beneath the very surface of the original Bible text. We have learned
that these amazing facts demonstrate that even every "jot" and
"tittle" (the smallest letter and the smallest mark) of the Bible is
inspired by God.

Dear reader, these newly discovered facts have a vital relationship to every human being. They affect each and every one
of us in a very definite way. Why? Because in proving the great
truth of the divine inspiration of the Bible, they place upon each
of us a certain responsibility—a responsibility which cannot be
avoided.

If we gain knowledge that the Bible is a supernatural, God-inspired book—the very Word of God Himself—a strange thing happens. Knowledge of this great truth never leaves us where it finds us—we never remain as we were before. Such knowledge **bestows a privilege, it opens an opportunity, and it creates a responsibility to examine and heed the instructions God has given us in His Word.**

Once we know that the Bible is God's Word, the issue can never end at that point. Merely acknowledging that the Bible is divine is not sufficient. If we are to be consistent and honest with ourselves, we must continue one step farther—we must learn and accept what God has to say concerning us in His Word. If the Bible were a mere human production, we would be under no obligation to give any special attention to it. However, inasmuch as it is divine, we cannot justly disregard its contents and we cannot casually lay it aside saying that it has no special relationship to us.

It is our duty to know, believe, and obey the instructions God has given in His Word.

The Bible gives God's message to all humanity. It tells us the purpose for which the Scriptures were written. It tells us why some cannot understand the Bible. It tells why some do not think as the Bible teaches. It tells why some dislike the Bible and why some condemn its teaching. Most important of all is the fact that it gives a perfect picture and description of ourselves—it enables us to see ourselves as we really are and enables us to know of our future.

When the Bible makes a statement, every word of that statement can be relied upon as true. Being of divine origin, it speaks with sovereign authority. It speaks without apology. The teachings of the Bible are not complicated and difficult to understand, for the Author of the Book, the Holy Spirit of God, promises that all who humbly come to its pages will be guided and enlightened in understanding its teachings.

There are various Bible statements which vitally concern our eternal well-being. Let us examine these statements in a spirit of honesty and truth.

Many have asked the question—

Why Was the Bible Written?

God clearly states His purpose in giving the Bible to mankind.

> **"Written that you might believe that Jesus is the Christ, the Son of God; and believing you might have life through his name." —John 20:31**

From this verse of Scripture, we learn that "life" is obtained through believing in Jesus Christ.

> **"that believing (in Jesus Christ) you might have life through his name."**

We shall learn that the "life" mentioned in this passage is not "physical life," but "spiritual life." The fact that we have physical life does not necessarily mean that we also have spiritual life for the Scripture bears out the strange truth that individuals may be alive physically and yet be "dead" spiritually.

> **"dead in your sins" —Colossians 2:13**

"dead in trespasses and sins" —Ephesians 2:1

"dead in sins," —Ephesians 2:5

"dead while she liveth" —1 Timothy 5:6

By nature, we are "dead" spiritually.

"Wherefore, as by one man sin entered into the world, and death by sin; and so death passed upon all men" —Romans 5:12; 2 Corinthians 5:14

By nature, we are "sinners."

"all have sinned" —Romans 5:12

"all (are) under sin" —Romans 3:9

"all have sinned and come short of the glory of God." —Romans 3:23

"the Scripture has concluded all under sin" —Galatians 3:22

"there is no man that sins not" —1 Kings 8:46

"there is not a just man upon the earth, that does good, and sins not." —Ecclesiastes 7:20

"There is none righteous, no, not one." —Romans 3:10

"If we say we have no sin we deceive ourselves."
—1 John 1:8

"If we say we have not sinned, we make him (Christ) a liar." —1 John 1:10

Sin is a sad and terrible reality. This fact is proved not only by the teaching of Scripture but also by the testimony of all mankind. All have been hounded by remorse of conscience for wrong-doing.

By nature, we are "lost."

We are "guilty before God." —Romans 3:19

We are "condemned already." —John 3:18

As sinners we are "unjust" in God's sight. —1 Peter 3:18

"There is not a just man upon the earth"
—Ecclesiastes 7:20

"There is none righteous, no not one." —Romans 3:10

Our hearts are "not right in the sight of God."
—Acts 8:21; Psalm 78:37

Our hearts are "deceitful . . . and desperately wicked"
—Jeremiah 17:9

By nature, we are "sold under sin" —Romans 7:14; Isaiah 52:3

We are the "servants of sin" —Romans 6:17; John 8:34

We are "holden (bound or held captive) by the cords of sin." —Proverbs 5:22

As sinners we are abiding in "darkness" —1 Peter 2:9; Ephesians 5:8

Sins "have separated" us from God. There is no communion or fellowship with Him —Isaiah 59:2

By nature, we are "far off" from God —Ephesians 2:13

and we are "lost" —Luke 19:10

We are "without Christ. . . . having no hope." —Ephesians 2:12

We are "without God in the world." —Ephesians 2:12

By nature, we are helpless and hopeless sinners. We are dead spiritually and are guilty and unjust before God. We are separated or alienated from God and have no communion or fellowship with Him. We are lost, "having no hope."

It is a precious truth to know that irrespective of our state and condition by nature—

God loves us.

"God commends his love toward us. . . . while we were yet sinners." —Romans 5:8

"Herein is love, not that we loved God, but that He loved us." —1 John 4:10

"In this was manifest the love of God toward us, because that God sent His only begotten Son into the world that we might live through Him." —1 John 4:9

"For God so loved the world, that he gave his only begotten Son, that whosoever believeth in him should not perish, but have everlasting life." —John 3:16

"Behold, what manner of love the Father hath bestowed upon us, that we should be called the sons of God." —1 John 3:1

For What Purpose Did the Son of God Come to This Earth?

Christ came to accomplish a definite work. He came to provide "salvation" for sinners.

"Jesus Christ came into the world to save sinners."
—1 Timothy 1:15

Christ "is come to seek and to save that which is lost."
—Luke 19:10; Matthew 11:18

"God sent . . . his Son into the world . . . that the world through him might be saved." —John 3:17; John 12:47

"The Father sent the Son to be the Saviour of the world." —1 John 4:14

Christ came "to make reconciliation for the sins of the people." —Hebrews 2:17

"God . . . sent his Son to be the propitiation for our sins." —1 John 4:10

"He was manifested to take away our sins." —1 John 3:5

"I am come that they might have life." —John 10:10

"God sent his only begotten Son into the world that we might live through him." —1 John 4:9

By Coming to This Earth How Did Christ Make It Possible for Sinners to Be "Saved?"

How did He accomplish the work which He came to do?

The Son of God did not accomplish this great work by coming to this earth to be a **"good example"** or a **"great religious teacher."** Neither did He accomplish this work by giving the world **"noble philosophical principles."** There is a far deeper meaning involved than this.

Christ, the sinless Son of God, as "a lamb without spot or blemish," gave Himself on the cross as a sacrifice for sin. He, the innocent party, became the sin- bearer for the guilty.

(I) By His Death on the Cross Christ became Our Saviour

"His own self bare our sins in his own body on the tree (cross)" —1 Peter 2:24

"He (God) has made Him (Christ) to be sin for us." —1 Corinthians 5:21

"The Lord (God) has laid on Him (Christ) the iniquity of us all." —Isaiah 53:6

"Christ died for the ungodly." —Romans 5:6

"While we were yet sinners Christ died for us." —Romans 5:8

"Christ hath once suffered for sins, the just (Christ) for the unjust (sinners)" —1 Peter 3:18. Also Titus 2:14, Galatians 1:4, 1 Corinthians 15:3, 1 Corinthians 5:21, 1 John 3:16.

(II) By His Death on the Cross Christ Shed His Blood for Us

(a) Through the shed blood of Christ
—We are "redeemed"

"Thou (Christ) wast slain and thou hast redeemed us to God by thy blood." —Revelation 5:9

"We have redemption through His blood."
—Colossians 1:14; Ephesians 1:7

**"Ye were not redeemed with corruptible things such
as silver or gold. . . . but (you were redeemed) with
the precious blood of Christ as of a lamb without spot
and without blemish." —1Peter 1:18–19**

**"You have sold yourselves for nought and you shall be
redeemed without money." —Isaiah 52:3**

**"By His own blood He . . . obtained eternal
redemption for us." —Hebrews 9:12**

Notice the following important truth in regard to "redemption."

**"You are not your own, For you are bought with a
price." —1 Corinthians 6:19–20**

**The Church of God Christ "has purchased with His
own blood." —Acts 20:28**

Christ "gave His life a ransom." —Matthew 20:28

He "gave Himself a ransom." —1 Timothy 2:6

These Scripture references using the words "redeemed," "ran-
somed," "bought," and "purchased" are particularly significant.

"Redeemed" means "bought back." Sinners are sold under sin
(Romans 6:17; Isaiah 52:3) but are redeemed by Christ's blood.
Sinners could be redeemed or purchased from their guilty, sin-
ful, lost, and condemned condition, only by some Person paying

the price. Christ paid the price to redeem sinners. The price which He paid was not silver or gold (1 Peter 1:18) or money (Isaiah 52:3) but was His own shed blood—His own life.

(b) Through the shed blood of Christ

—We have the "forgiveness" or "remission" of our sins

"My blood of the new testament (covenant) is shed for many for the remission of sins." —Matthew 26:28

"In whom we have redemption through His (Christ's) blood, the forgiveness of sins." —Ephesians 1:7; Colossians 1:14

(c) Through the shed blood of Christ

—We are cleansed from sin

"Jesus Christ . . . loved us, and washed us from our sins in His own blood." —Revelation 1:5

"The blood of Jesus Christ His (God's) Son cleanseth us from all sin." —2 John 1:7

(d) Through the shed blood of Christ

—We are "justified" (made "just") before God and are "reconciled" to God.

"Being now justified by His own blood." —Romans 5:9

"When we were yet enemies, we were reconciled to God by the death of His Son." —Romans 5:10

(e) Through the shed blood of Christ

—We are made "nigh" to God

> "But now in Christ Jesus ye who sometimes were
> far off are made nigh (brought close to God) by the
> blood of Christ." —Ephesians 2:13

(f) Through the shed blood of Christ

—**We make peace with God**

> "Having made peace through the blood of His Cross."
> —Colossians 1:20

We have seen what **Christ has done** to provide for our salvation, now—

What must we do to be saved?

The Bible teaches that this salvation cannot be earned or merited by good works or deeds.

> **"Not by works of righteousness which we have done,
> but according to His mercy He saved us." —Titus 3:5**

> **"saved . . . not of works, lest any man should boast."
> —Ephesians 2:8**

> **"Who hath saved us . . . not according to works."
> —2 Timothy 1:8**

> **Our good works or our righteousness will not obtain
> salvation for us, for our "righteousness is as filthy
> rags in His sight." —Isaiah 64:6**

Salvation is the "gift of God" therefore it cannot be earned or merited. If we could earn our own salvation, it would not have been necessary for Christ to have died.

Alas, how many depend upon their own self-righteousness for salvation. Many depend upon their church membership. Others depend upon their good living—in being respectable citizens of the community, in supporting their families, and in contributing to the poor, and to the upkeep of the church.

A way of salvation which a person devises for himself, even though there is much good about it, will never bring the soul to God.

Man's way of salvation by "works" is not God's way.

> "There is a way that seems right unto a man, but the end thereof are the ways of death." —Proverbs 14:12

> "My thoughts are not your thoughts, neither are your ways my ways, says the Lord. For as the heavens are higher than the earth, so are my ways higher than your ways, and my thoughts than your thoughts." —Isaiah 55:8–9

We Are Saved by Faith—By Believing in Christ's Finished Work of Redemption, and by Receiving Him as Our Personal Saviour

(a) We must believe in the work of Christ.

> "Believe on the Lord Jesus Christ, and thou shall be saved." —Acts 16:31

> "Through His name whosoever believes in him shall receive the remission of sins." —Acts 10:43

> **"And by him all that believe are justified from all things." —Acts 13:39**

> **"Without faith it is impossible to please God." —Hebrews 11:6**

Genuine faith in the work of Christ will be accompanied by repentance.

> **"God commands all men everywhere to repent." —Acts 17:30**

> **"Godly sorrow works repentance to salvation." —2 Corinthians 7:9–10**

The words of the publican express the thought.

> **"God be merciful to me a sinner." —Luke 18:13**

> **"If we confess our sins, He is faithful and just to forgive us our sins, and to cleanse us from all unrighteousness." —1 John 1:9**

> **"Repent . . . for the remission of sins." —Acts 2:38**

> **"Repent . . . that your sins may be blotted out." —Acts 3:19**

> **"Except you repent you shall all likewise perish." —Luke 13:3**

(b) We must receive Christ as our personal Saviour.
By nature, we are "dead" spiritually. To become alive spiritually we must be born of God. We must be "born again." As we can

enter this world only by the process of a natural birth, so we can enter the kingdom of God only by the process of a spiritual birth. Spiritual life is received only by the spiritual birth.

> **"That which is born of the flesh is flesh and that which is born of the Spirit is spirit" (John 3:6.**

> **To be saved—to be a child of God—we must be "born of God." —John 1:13**

> **Christ said, "Verily, verily I say unto you except a man be born again he cannot see the kingdom of God." —John 3:3**

Regeneration, or the "new birth" is not baptism, or confirmation, neither is it reformation. Regeneration is not the old nature altered, reformed, or re-invigorated. It is not a reforming process on the part of man, and it is not a natural forward step in man's development. Regeneration is a new birth from above, and is a supernatural creative act on the part of God. The sinner receives a new nature—God's nature, and he is a new creature, and puts on the new man which God creates after holiness and righteousness.

> **"A new heart will I give you, and a new spirit will I put within you;"—Ezekiel 36:26**

> **"If any man be in Christ, he is a new creature; old things pass away and behold all things become new." —2 Corinthians 5:17; Ephesians 4:24**

By regeneration, or new birth, we are admitted into the kingdom of God. There is no other way of becoming a believer but by being born from above. Too often we find other things, such as good works, reformation, or baptism, substituted by man for God's appointed way of becoming a child of God. To be a child of God one must be born of the Spirit of God.

> **Jesus said, "Except a man be born again he cannot see the kingdom of God." —John 3:3**

No age, sex, position, or condition exempts anyone from this necessity. Not to be born again is to be lost. There is no substitute for the new birth. Paul said, "Neither circumcision avails anything nor uncircumcision, but **a new creature**" (Galations 6:15 emphasis added). That is the all-important thing, being a new creature in Christ. Christ did not say that you ought to be born again, or it would be good for you to be born again. He said, "You must be born again" (John 3:7).

We can experience this new birth by receiving Christ as our personal Saviour.

John 1:12 tells us, "As many as received Him [Christ] to them gave He power to become the sons [children] of God, even to them that believe on His name."

We cannot receive eternal life without receiving Christ. "God hath given to us eternal life, and **this life is in His Son**, he that has the Son has life, and he that has not the Son of God has not life" (1 John 5:11–12 emphasis added).

> **"Verily, verily, I say unto you, He that believes on me hath everlasting life." —John 6:47**

We will experience this new birth—we will be born of God—if we receive Christ as our Saviour. We will be new creatures in Christ Jesus, "and old things will pass away and behold all things will become new" (2 Corinthians 5:17). Christ will dwell in us (Galatians 2:20). And we "shall not come into condemnation (judgement) but are passed from **death** unto **life**" (John 5:24).

One of the most wonderful facts about this salvation is that it is for **everyone.** "God is no respecter of persons" (Acts 10:34). "**Whosoever** shall call upon the name of the Lord shall be saved" (Acts 2:21). Christ encouragingly calls, "Come unto Me all you that labor and are heavy laden and I will give you rest" (Matthew 11:28). "Him that comes unto Me I will in no wise cast out" (John 6:37, Revelation 3:20; 22:17).

We can know that we are saved, and we can know Christ as our personal Saviour. 1 John 5:10 says, "He that believes on the Son of God hath the **witness** within himself." Romans 8:16 says, "The Spirit itself bears witness with our spirit that we are the children of God."

Dear reader, there is no middle territory; you are either saved or you are not saved. The Bible says, "No servant can serve two masters. . . . ye cannot serve God and mammon" (Luke 16:13). Christ said, "He that is not with Me is against Me" (Luke 11:23). "Know ye not, that to whom you yield yourselves servants to obey, his servants you are to whom you obey: whether of sin unto death, or of obedience unto righteousness?" (Romans 6:16).

The Bible also says, "Choose ye this day whom you shall serve" (Joshua 24:15).

"Now is the accepted time, now is the day of salvation." —2 Corinthians 6:2

"Today if ye hear His voice, harden not your hearts." —Hebrews 3:7

Do not postpone accepting Christ. "Seek you the Lord while He may be found, call upon Him while He is near." —Isaiah 55:6

"You know not what shall be on the morrow." —James 4:14

"For what shall it profit a man, if he shall gain the whole world, and lose his own soul? Or what shall a man give in exchange for his soul?" —Matthew 16:26

"Come now, and let us reason together, saith the Lord: though your sins be as scarlet, they shall be as white as snow; though they be red like crimson, they shall be as wool." —Isaiah 1:18.

"This is a faithful saying, and worthy of all acceptation, that Christ came into the world to save sinners; of whom I am chief." —I Timothy 1:15

Why Are Men Lost?

"Because they believe not on Me." —John 16:9

"He that believes not the Son shall not see life: but the wrath of God abides on him." —John 3:36

Complete Salvation: Yshuwah or Sozo

*I*N THE PREVIOUS SECTION, Karl Sabiers talked about the salvation of a person's spirit, or being born again. The Hebrew word for "salvation" is *Yshuwah*, which can variously mean deliverance, help, salvation, and welfare encompassing the wellbeing of spirit, soul, and body. Similarly, the Greek words for "salvation" are *sozo* and *soteria*, which actually include the salvation of a person's spirit, soul, and body. In Philippians 2:12, "work out your salvation [*soteria*] with fear and trembling," Paul is referring to the salvation of the soul. Whereas the salvation of a person's spirit happens instantaneously at the second birth, the soul is being refined and made holy throughout the believer's life. Similarly, 1 Peter 1:9, "receiving the outcome of your faith— the salvation [*soteria*] of your souls," also talks about the transformation of the soul. *Soteria* can refer to physical survival or health as seen in Acts 27:34, "Therefore, I urge you to take some food—for this is for your survival [*soteria*], since not one of you will lose a hair from his head." Consistently, the word refers to physical safety and deliverance from danger in Philippians 1:19: "for I know that this will turn out for my deliverance [*soteria*]."

The word *sozo* has a similar range of meaning, including eternal salvation, physical safety, and healing. *Sozo* refers to eternal, spiritual salvation in several passages: In Matthew 1:21, "For He [*Yeshua*] will save [*sozo*] His people from their sins"; Acts 2:47, "And every day the Lord was adding to their number those being saved [*sozo*]"; and in Romans 8:24, "For in hope we were saved [*sozo*]," the word "salvation" means eternal spiritual life. In James 1:21, "salvation" means the soul's redemption. James admonishes people to put off all evil and receive the Word of God, "which is able to save [*sozo*] your souls." *Sozo*, like *soteria*, is used in the sense of safety and deliverance from physical danger. In Matthew 8:25, the disciples asked Yeshua to save [*sozo*] them from a storm, and in Luke 23:35 and John 12:27, *sozo* refers to the possibility of Yeshua being saved from the trials ahead of Him. Additionally, *sozo* is used in direct reference to physical healing: In Matthew 9:22, Yeshua healed a sick woman and stated that her faith had made her well [*sozo*], and in James 5:15, *sozo* refers to being saved from sickness by the prayer of faith.

Indeed, Yeshua's ministry of salvation, summed up in Isaiah 61:1, included healing the brokenhearted and setting the spiritual and physical captives free. In Isaiah 53:4–5, it was foretold that the Messiah would bear our griefs, our sicknesses, our transgressions, and our iniquity. Thus, whatever our need is, Yeshua has it covered. Philippians 4:19 reads, "My God will supply every need of yours according to the riches of His glory in Messiah Yeshua." In John 14:14, Yeshua said that if we ask anything in His name He will do it, and in John 15:7, He said that if we abide in Him and His Word, anything we wish will be granted us.

Perhaps one of the most profound statements in the Bible is that Yeshua came to destroy the works of the devil (see 1 John 3:8). Many people think that God is in charge of this world, however, Yeshua clearly stated that the devil is the ruler of this world (see John 14:30). Yeshua said in John 10:10 that the thief (the devil) comes to steal, kill, and destroy, but that He has come to give us life. For those who believe in Yeshua, any work of the devil, be it lack of faith, sickness, danger, poverty, spiritual or temporal oppression, lingering grief, or mental anguish can be overcome through faith, perseverance, prayer, and the use of authority. Yeshua, when dying at Golgotha, uttered the words, "It is finished."

Bibliography

Biltz, M. (2014). *Blood Moons: Decoding the Imminent Heavenly Signs*. WND Books.

Jeffrey, G. R. (1998). *Mysterious Bible Codes*. Word Publishing.

Heflin, J. (2021). 10,5,6,5. YHWH. DNA. Retrieved from https://www.youtube.com/watch?v=KH-oT_PaaQQ

Israeli Scientists Find God's Name (YHWH) in our D.N.A.–We Are His from the Beginning (2021). Retrieved from https://www.youtube.com/watch?v=MkoB8WfqMls

Meldau, F. J. (2017). *The Prophets Still Speak: Messiah in Both Testaments*. The Friends of Israel Gospel Ministry.

Michelson, D. (n.d.). *Reading the Torah with Equal Intervals: A Review*. Retrieved from https://www.answering-islam.org/Religions/Numerics/torah.html

Panin, I. (1934). *The Shorter Works of Ivan Panin*. The Association of the Covenant People.

Ordman, D. (2020). *Rabbi David Ordman: Torah Codes, Part 1*. Retrieved from https://www.youtube.com/watch?v=F7ArJm8heo8

Rambsel, Y. (2000). *The Genesis Factor*. Lion's Head Publishing.

Sabiers, K. (1941). *Mathematics Proves Holy Scriptures*. New England Bible Sales.

Stanton, D. (n.d.). *Amazing Discoveries. God's Numerical Design in Creation and His Word*. Maranatha Revival Crusade.

Retrieved from https://www.maranathamrc.com/BOOKS.htm

TES. Bible Software. https://jewishsoftware.com/download-bible-codes-the-keys-to-the-bible

Vedder, M., & Thompson, J. (2014). *Ivan Panin's Numerics in Scripture.* New England Bible Sales.

Witztum, D. Rips, E., & Rosenberg, Y. (1994). "Equidistant Letter Sequences in the Book of Genesis." *Statistical Science, 9*(3), 429-438.

If You Enjoyed This Book, Please Tell Others…

- Post a 5-Star review on Amazon.

- Write about the book on your Facebook, Twitter, Instagram page—any social media you regularly use!

- If you have led a group study or participated in one using this book, share that experience too.

- If you blog, consider referencing the book, your study experiences, or publishing an excerpt from the book with a link to my website. You have my permission to do this as long as you provide proper credit and backlinks.

- Recommend the book to friends. Word-of-mouth is still the most effective form of advertising.

- Purchase additional copies to give as gifts.

You can find us on the web at:
ShoahSurvivors.com

www.ingramcontent.com/pod-product-compliance
Lightning Source LLC
Chambersburg PA
CBHW060237030426
42335CB00014B/1496

9 781941 512609